Bridgebuilding

Bridgebuilding

*Making Peace with Conflict
in the Church*

Alastair McKay

CANTERBURY
PRESS
Norwich

© Alastair McKay 2019

First published in 2019 by the Canterbury Press Norwich
Editorial office
3rd Floor, Invicta House
108–114 Golden Lane
London EC1Y 0TG, UK
www.canterburypress.co.uk

Canterbury Press is an imprint of Hymns Ancient & Modern Ltd
(a registered charity)

H
Y
M **Ancient**
N **&Modern** EST 1861
S

Hymns Ancient & Modern® is a registered trademark of
Hymns Ancient & Modern Ltd
13A Hellesdon Park Road, Norwich,
Norfolk NR6 5DR, UK

British Library Cataloguing in Publication data

A catalogue record for this book is available
from the British Library

978 1 78622 141 4

Typeset by Manila Typesetting Company
Printed and bound in Great Britain by
CPI Group (UK) Ltd

Contents

Acknowledgements   ix

About CPAS   xi

Foreword   xiii

Introduction   xv

1 **What is Conflict Doing in God's World?**   1
   Dialogue with Rachel Treweek   5
   Theological reflection: Genesis 1,
   Revelation 21 (Creation and re-creation)   8

2 **Know Thyself – and Value Others**   10
   Dialogue with Colin Patterson   17
   Theological reflection: 1 Corinthians 12
   (Paul's understanding of the body of Christ)   20

3 **Grow in Emotional Maturity**   22
   Dialogue with Liz Holdsworth   29
   Theological reflection: Ephesians 4.1–16
   (Growing into maturity in Christ)   33

4 **Be Real about Power**   35
   Dialogue with Rosemarie Davidson-Gotobed   43
   Theological reflection: Matthew 26.57–68
   (Jesus on trial before the High Priest)   46

5 **Use Good Theory**   48
   Dialogue with Lia Shimada   55
   Theological reflection: Acts 6.1–11
   (Conflict in the early church)   59

6   Shepherd the Process   62
     Dialogue with Joanna Williams   69
     Theological reflection: Luke 24.13–35
     (The walk to Emmaus)   73

7   Make Space for Feelings, Silence and Touch   75
     Dialogue with Frank White   82
     Theological reflection: Matthew 17.1–8
     (The transfiguration of Jesus)   86

8   Recognize the Limits   88
     Dialogue with Sandra Cobbin   97
     Theological reflection: Acts 15.36–41
     (Paul's split with Barnabas)   100

9   Love Your Enemy   103
     Dialogue with Sarah Hills   114
     Theological reflection: Matthew 5.38–48
     (On avoiding retaliation or taking revenge)   117

10   Build a Culture Together   120
     Dialogue with Ernie Whalley   130
     Theological reflection: Acts 2.42–47
     (Practices that shape communities of peace)   132

11   Observe the Peacemakers   135
     Dialogue with Joe Campbell   143
     Theological reflection: John 21.15–19
     (Jesus restores Peter)   147

12   Build Bridges to Heaven   150
     Dialogue with and theological reflection
     by Sam Wells   157

Further Resources   162

For Sue, with my thanks, admiration and love.
And for Eleanor and James, with my prayers
for God's blessing.

Acknowledgements

I am deeply grateful to Colin Patterson for his invaluable feedback, comment and editorial suggestions. This book is immeasurably better for his contribution.

I am grateful to an old friend, Jonathan Steele, who carefully proof-read each chapter and picked up various glitches. And to Br Thomas OSB, the Abbot of Mucknell Abbey, who kindly read some chapters and provided useful comment.

I am deeply indebted to Rachel Treweek, Liz Holdsworth, Colin Patterson, Rosemarie Davidson-Gotobed, Lia Shimada, Jo Williams, Frank White, Sandra Cobbin, Sarah Hills, Ernie Whalley, Joe Campbell and Sam Wells, my conversation partners for this book. Each has been a blessing and an inspiration, and their contributions profoundly enrich the book.

I also want to thank the following.

My early Mennonite mediator mentors: Ron Kraybill, John Paul Lederach, Richard Blackburn, Carolyn Schrock-Shenk, David Brubaker and Kirsten Zerger. I would not be a bridge-builder without their inspiring examples, outstanding teaching and gracious encouragement. I am especially grateful to John Paul and Carolyn who agreed to be interviewed for Chapter 11. Sadly, Carolyn died as the book manuscript was being finalized.

My former colleagues at Bridge Builders: Colin Patterson, Charletta Erb, Sharon Kniss, Sam Moyer, Michelle Power and Sarah Wilkin; and the many staff at the former London Mennonite Centre, beginning with Alan and Eleanor Kreider. The development of Bridge Builders' training courses and intervention services was the fruit of a stimulating partnership together over many years. It was a joy to work with such colleagues, along with a wider group of associate trainers and mediators.

Ric Thorpe, now Bishop of Islington, who urged me to write a book about bridge-building.

Sam Wells, Vicar of St Martin-in-the-Fields, who took me on as his curate in 2015. I have learnt more about Christian ministry than I can say from him. At St Martin's I was privileged to serve with and learn from a dynamic clergy team comprising Sam, Richard Carter, Katherine Hedderly and Jonathan Evens.

James Lawrence, the Leadership Principal at CPAS, and his team who did wonderful work in bringing to publication my *Growing Bridgebuilders* training resource in 2016. I am thankful that James' ongoing commitment led to CPAS deciding to co-publish this book with Canterbury Press.

Christine Smith, Publishing Director at Canterbury Press, and her team for their guidance and encouragement in bringing the book to publication.

Sue McKay, who has patiently endured my travails, and whose faithful support helped bring the book to completion.

About CPAS

CPAS enables churches to help every person in the UK and Republic of Ireland hear and discover the good news of Jesus Christ.

Local church mission is the heartbeat of CPAS. As an Anglican evangelical mission agency we believe the message of the cross is real and relevant to all people, and that effective local church ministry is key to seeing women, men, young people and children come to faith in Christ.

We make mission possible by developing Christian leaders through leadership training, equipping churches with much needed resources to help them grow, running over 90 Venture and Falcon holidays for thousands of eight to 18 year olds each year, and appointing clergy through our patronage work.

Our training for leaders includes the Arrow Leadership Programme, training events for ordained and lay leaders on a wide variety of topics related to missional leadership (often in partnership with dioceses), and resources for churches to use, including Growing Leaders, Mentoring Matters, PCC Tonight and Talk Calling.

www.cpas.org.uk
Facebook.com/CPASNews
Twitter: @CPASLeadership, @CPASNews

Foreword

It is bold to claim that 'reconciliation is the gospel', as this book does. But it should be less controversial to assert that our work at reconciliation needs to begin in the Church. However, as Christians, our track record in handling our tensions is far from glowing. The fractured body of Christ on earth is testimony to that. Christians have been disagreeing since the beginning. The Gospels are painfully honest in their record: Jesus' first disciples fought among themselves. They argued about who was the greatest, and who should exercise most influence. Jesus challenged the disciples about this; and modelled a different way. After Jesus' resurrection and ascension, the early Church went on to bicker over how to properly include minorities and the neediest in their community. And then to have a protracted dispute over including Gentile believers. The Holy Spirit inspired them to find creative ways forward. Encouragingly, the Spirit continues such work among us today, as this book testifies.

I first met Alastair McKay six years ago while I was a Canon at Salisbury Cathedral. I knew of Bridge Builders' reputation for equipping church leaders with vision and skills for bridge-building. The course I undertook has equipped my ministry in a range of settings for which I have been grateful. I warmed to Alastair's passion for this ministry; and am glad he has now shared some of his learning in this book. Alastair delights in working collaboratively with others. I appreciate the deep wisdom that emerges from his conversations with his dialogue partners and other peacemakers, woven through these chapters. This makes for a rich feast.

I am therefore pleased to commend this book most heartily to all those wanting to do better at handling the tensions among us in the Church. We need all the help we can get. This book offers plenty.

The Rt Revd and Rt Hon. Sarah Mullally, Bishop of London

Introduction

This book largely emerges from personal experience, and in this introduction I want to tell something of the story of how I became a 'bridge-builder'. I will then explain who the book is intended for and how it is structured; before concluding with a note about some of the stories that I share.

Bridge-building: a defining metaphor

At 30 years old I was despondent: I had resolved to leave the Civil Service by this age but was still there. Having explored several different roads, including Bible college and missionary work, I had drawn a blank. I still did not know what I was called to.

It was February 1994, and I was sitting in the chapel of the London Mennonite Centre with two dozen other people. We were beginning a course of training led by Ron Kraybill, a Mennonite mediator. My world was about to change and take a whole new direction.

My wife Sue and I had met Ron four years before. We had been put in touch by Ron's brother, Nelson, newly appointed director of the London Mennonite Centre. Visiting Ron and his family was the start of a firm friendship. I really liked Ron. I could not express it then, but deep down I wanted to be like him.

Ron was a North American, who had been sent to South Africa by a Mennonite peace agency. He was part of a movement of conciliators trying to ensure a peaceful transition to democratic rule by the black-majority peoples. There was hope. Mandela had been released from prison, and his political party, the ANC, was unbanned. But the road to a peaceful society was far from assured. Ron was offering training to diverse groups, including members of the police force, politicians and community activists, in the hope of contributing to a lasting peace, and avoiding an outpouring of bloodshed, seen too often across the African continent in other transitions of power.

This was experience Ron brought to leading a three-day course in London, an introduction to a mediation process. I was sitting there, and, by the end of the first day, I was electrified: I loved the process we were being taught and the way we were being instructed: experientially, by practising what we were learning. This was fun! By the end of the course I had arranged with Nelson that we would ask for volunteers to sign up with their details if they were interested to be involved in establishing a new mediation project in London.

Several people signed up, including myself and Nelson. I knew that this field was the one in which I wanted to set my plough. Some called it mediation. Others called it conflict resolution. I just knew that this was 'it' for me. Over the following weeks, our small group met several times. Half a dozen kept coming. We had different ideas about what sort of project to set up. After discussion, we reached consensus over establishing a community mediation service in the London Borough of Haringey, where the Mennonite Centre and the Wood Green Mennonite Church were both located.

We also needed a name. The obvious option was to call the project Haringey Community Mediation Service. But I wanted a name that would paint a picture of what the project was about, not just give a description and, in the middle of the night, it came to me: 'Bridge Builders'.

Over the next few months it became clear that our community mediation project was unviable. Our infrastructure was a telephone line in the Mennonite Centre, a basic paper flyer, and just two people, Nelson and I, who were willing to mediate a live case. We both had our hands full, being two of the three 'elders' leading the Wood Green Mennonite Church. Nelson was busy directing the established programmes of the Mennonite Centre, and I had a demanding job in Whitehall. Having launched the community mediation service in February 1995, we concluded before the end of that year that we needed to close it down.

Out of the ashes arose the project that Nelson and I had dreamed of at the outset: a service of the Mennonite Centre that looked to fill what we saw as a gaping hole in British society. It would serve the British churches. It would help church leaders to grasp that transforming conflict was integral to the gospel of Jesus Christ and emerged from that gospel. We secured a grant from a Mennonite agency to pilot the initiative at the Centre in London, which the Centre's trustees approved, and I began working a day a week leading the new Bridge Builders project, alongside Nelson.

I did not realize, in the middle of that revelatory night, that the bridge-building metaphor would come to define so much of my working life. But it has, and this book is my attempt to distil some learning from the last quarter of a century.

Who this book is intended for

The primary audience are Christians in the British Isles. Whether you are a lay person in the church or an ordained minister, in Britain or in Ireland, this book is intended for you. If you think those of us in the Church might improve how we handle our differences, if you wonder whether there are better ways of engaging with our conflicts, then read on.

It is also hoped that the book will be of interest to Christians across the English-speaking world, with similar concerns. If that is you, then please be mindful that you may need to do some translation for your context.

Whatever your setting, I believe that, as fellow Christians, as the body of Christ, we are called to the ministry of reconciliation. And that means finding ways to face into our disagreements and tensions, and to navigate a way through conflict. If you share that conviction, then I hope that this book will be of service to you on the journey. And I also hope that you might find some others with whom you can read and discuss the book: your learning will be deeper, if so.

There is plenty to learn. Some of what you read may be familiar already, but I hope you will discover some pleasant surprises, useful stimulation and hopeful inspiration along the way – and at least the occasional new insight.

How the chapters are structured

Each chapter deals with an action you can take to contribute to bridge-building and to making peace with conflict in the Church – and beyond. This is the usual pattern:

- Reflections on the topic.
- Further thoughts from one of my conversation partners, in response to some tailored questions, written up in a more informal, conversational manner.
- A short theological reflection, focused on a biblical text.

To help readers discuss the book with others, questions for individual reflection and small group discussion are available on my website at www.alastairmckay.com/writing.

A note on the stories shared

A number of delicate true stories are included. In two of them, people's identities are used with their permission: Simon and Natalie in Chapter 6; and Jonathan in Chapter 10. A few of the stories are on public record, such as that of Jo Berry and Pat Magee in Chapter 9. Some stories are my recollections of encounters with fellow bridge-builders and peacemakers, and others speak about clergy and churches I have worked with, whose identities are concealed.

In some cases, stories are based on either an amalgam or a simplification of real people and events, using fictionalized names. They are not an attempt to render faithfully the details of individuals or settings; rather they are intended to capture their truth and essence. This is important to remember, if the reader thinks they might recognize something of themselves or their situation in a story told here.

I

What is Conflict Doing
in God's World?

How are we to understand the place of conflict in God's world?
I want to tell two stories of how I first encountered some insights
that have profoundly shaped my thinking.

New thinking

I have been inspired in the field of conflict transformation by a
Mennonite trainer called Carolyn Schrock-Shenk. I met Carolyn
when I was studying at Eastern Mennonite University in 1998.
Hearing her speak, I admired her passion, courage and honesty as she explored conflict and differences between people. In
1999, while I was an intern with a Mennonite peace centre in
Chicago, Carolyn approached me about contributing to a book
she was co-editing entitled *Making Peace with Conflict*. Over 20
different Mennonite practitioners from the conflict transformation field were invited to contribute, and I proposed writing a
chapter on congregational decision-making and building group
consensus.

I submitted my chapter and then heard nothing from the
editors, until I was sent proofs. They made distressing reading. A story of events in my congregation in London had been
substantially altered and was no longer faithful to my experience. Carolyn's co-editor had made these changes, but they
had not been run past me, and because the publication process was so advanced, it was difficult to restore the story to

something I could live with. But after a good deal of toing and froing – and some angst – we agreed a way forward. Painfully, I had discovered how significant a person's story is to them; and how much hangs on the way it is framed.

There was a certain irony in facing some conflict over a book that was all about finding better ways to handle conflict. Afterwards, Carolyn and I sought to be reconciled. We tried doing this by email, then in its infancy. And I learnt another painful lesson: email correspondence is *not* a good way of trying to bring healing and reconciliation, especially when there are strong feelings about what has happened. It was only some months later, when Carolyn and I met face-to-face at a national conflict-resolution conference, that we found a way of acknowledging one another's experience, and of bringing the measure of peace that was needed on both sides.

When *Making Peace with Conflict* was published, I read Carolyn's opening chapter.[1] It was a moment when the scales fell from my eyes. I was struck by her simple definition, that 'conflict equals differences plus tension'. It seemed novel to suggest that as soon as we experience discomfort and tension over our differences, we are touching conflict. It was a much broader definition than I was used to, but full of insight. I have employed it ever since. Two further thoughts from Carolyn struck me particularly.

The first is that conflict is an opportunity to know another person at a deeper level. I found that with the friction over my book chapter: I got to know and to appreciate Carolyn better. Although it had been painful, I came to treasure her in a more significant way than previously and was grateful for the person I discovered. This led me to extend a subsequent invitation, which I talk about in Chapter 11.

The second insight Carolyn provided through her writing is that conflict is natural, and is built into the fabric of creation.[2] Reflecting on the creation story in the opening chapter of Genesis, she suggested that in making such a diverse world, God was wiring it for conflict. Given such diversity, we are bound to bump up against one another in uncomfortable ways. We therefore need to expect conflict as a normal part of the territory of life itself. I should therefore not have been surprised that we had encountered some level of conflict in assembling a book on the subject. It might have been more surprising if we had not done so.

Accepting conflict as an integral part of God's good creation was a challenge to my previous assumption that conflict is a fruit of the fallen, sinful world. Carolyn's view was that conflict predated the entrance of sin. Conflict was therefore not innately bad or sinful. How we *respond* to the conflicts we face is what determines whether sin gets a foothold in the situation. But conflict itself is neither good nor bad, it is simply a reality of creation: tension over our differences. This offered a whole new light on the subject, which I eagerly shared with others in the years that followed, through Bridge Builders' training courses: conflict is a normal and natural part of the way that God has made the world.

Deeper thinking

Some 15 years later, my thinking was stretched further. For several years, I had been part of a group that met together occasionally to explore how mediation could be used within the Church of England. The group had been started by Stephen Ruttle, a barrister who had launched a community mediation service in conjunction with his local parish church. After many meetings, the group eventually agreed that we wanted to host a national conference to help get mediation and conflict resolution more firmly in the minds of Christians and church leaders in England. We agreed that the best location for this would be Coventry Cathedral, given its long-standing commitment to the work of reconciliation. It helped that one of our number, David Porter, then the Cathedral's Canon for Reconciliation, was enthusiastic about hosting the event.

The purpose of the conference, entitled 'Faith in Conflict', was twofold: to help the Church understand the challenge we faced arising from the inherited culture of how conflict is handled in churches; and to offer a new vision of handling conflict better. The planning group held a long discussion over who we might invite to deliver the key-note address. I suggested that we consider an ordained couple, Sam and Jo Wells, who had recently returned to the UK after several years working in the USA. Most of the group, being professional mediators, had not heard of them, and so were unenthusiastic. But a strong endorsement from Justin Welby, then Bishop of Durham, who had been involved since his time at Coventry Cathedral, swung the mood in favour.

The wisdom of having Sam and Jo address the Faith in Conflict conference became evident when we heard each of them speak. Jo gave us some deep insight into the place of lament in the journey of engaging with human loss and conflict, drawing on her Old Testament expertise. But it was Sam's presentation that particularly stretched my own thinking. Two points grabbed me most.

First, was recognizing that conflict is not restricted to this life but is part of our promised future. Heaven, Sam proposed, is a place of diversity and difference: it is not a conflict-free zone. Which means we will still have to address tension over our differences in heaven. The big change is that we will find continuously creative and constructive ways of doing so, that bear interesting new fruit. And that is partly because, 'Peace isn't the absence of conflict, but the transformation from destructive tension into dynamic creativity.'[3]

The second wonderful insight was seeing reconciliation as the very heart of the gospel. 'Far from being an essential, tiresome, and time-consuming precursor to the gospel, reconciliation *is* the gospel. There isn't anything more important to which reconciliation is but the prologue.'[4] I had always thought that the work of reconciliation mattered. Now I grasped why, in a new way. Reconciliation *is* the gospel: transforming conflict is the very business of God.

A conversation with Rachel Treweek

Rachel is the Bishop of Gloucester and was the first woman to be appointed as a diocesan bishop in the Church of England. She has participated in many Bridge Builders courses in the past and is on their Council of Reference.

Who or what has most shaped your understanding of conflict?
From a young age, the forming of relationships and living with a diverse group of people has been important to me. This influenced my decision to become a speech and language therapist: good communication is core to meaningful relationships. Working with children, families and teachers, I recognized the importance of understanding the individual as being located within a complex 'system' of relationships and connectedness. Then, after some family therapy training, my awareness of tension and conflict grew.

Although my calling to ordination seemingly 'interrupted' my family therapy plans, I began to see that I was being called to use my training in a different context. I had a renewed excitement about the interconnectedness of the body of Christ and how I could bring insights from family therapy to ordained ministry.

I attended theological college during the debates around women being ordained to the priesthood in the Church of England, debates eventually settled by a vote in General Synod in 1992. Staff and students alike held intense and opposing views. It was challenging for me to be a single woman living in community with people who held such strong views about whether I was being faithful to God. I therefore wanted to explore how to live in relationship with others amidst conflict, without compromising my own integrity or sense of justice.

Years later, as an Archdeacon, I was stimulated by the opportunities my role gave me to explore and engage with conflict within worshipping communities. This led me to undertake studies in group facilitation and conflict resolution, at a key time in the Church of England's journey of considering the consecration of women as bishops. As a member of General Synod, I found it a bruising time: conflict was rarely lived well. I was frustrated by the lack of places of encounter within our adversarial forum. So, I tried to build relationships and talk with people who held very different views from my own. Whilst we didn't agree with each other's perspectives, I was grateful for an experience of a deepening of love and connection, in a place of pain and frustration.

The introduction of facilitated conversations within the synodical process led to a significant shift. It brought us to the place of Synod voting in favour of women being consecrated to the episcopate. For me, the key factor was the enabling of safe human encounter amidst our differences. Creating places for conversation is not about trying to change other people's viewpoints, but rather about placing a high value on relationship at times of vehement disagreement. It's about endeavouring to deepen trust in our encounters – which is more about listening than speaking. It's also about staying connected, being honest and vulnerable, and not walking away from one another in the face of immense differences.

Now, as a bishop, the pectoral cross I often wear is made of bullet casings from the civil war in Mozambique. It was given to me by the Bishop of Lebombo and created by a project called 'Transforming Arms into Ploughshares' (Isa. 2.4). For me, it's a symbol of God's reconciling mission.

What, for you, have been significant insights in understanding the place of conflict in God's world?
I see conflict as a normal part of living in a world of rich diversity, in which no two people are the same, yet all are wonderfully made in the image of God. I hold fast to the truth that we are made to live in relationship with God, fellow human beings and the created world. And I believe that every experience of brokenness in our world involves a broken relationship, whether it be with God, people or creation. When I talk about this with a group, I reach upwards as a sign of being created to live in relationship with God, and then stretch out my arms to indicate our relationship with fellow human beings, and then point towards the ground as a sign of being in relationship with creation. It's no

coincidence that this forms the shape of a cross – because at the heart of God's mission is reconciliation (Col. 1.18–20). As a follower of Jesus, my hope is in the vision that one day all will be made new. In the present, creation is groaning, longing for liberation and wholeness (Rom. 8.18–21). But one day God's work of transformation and restoration will be complete (Rev. 21.1–5). And it's my desire to join in with what God is doing that's led me to be committed to the work of transforming conflict.

What difference has your evolving understanding of conflict made to the way you approach life and ministry?

My starting place is that conflict is a natural part of living in a world marked by difference, both beautiful and ugly. So, conflict is not something to be avoided. Whilst I cannot pretend that I enjoy conflict, I'm committed to engaging with it and want to communicate my desire to remain in relationship with others, even when I profoundly disagree with them.

In the early days of my ministry as Bishop of Gloucester I was intentional about giving time to situations of conflict, including being present with people for whom my appointment as their bishop prompted unease or dismay. In those conversations, I was unapologetic about my calling and role; yet I was also clear that I desire the flourishing and well-being of all people and wish to stay connected with them.

When I find myself in a place of conflict or needing to address conflictual situations, I'm learning to see that these are not inconvenient obstacles that have interrupted life, but are part of the normal ebb and flow – and need to be approached without undue anxiety or pressure. Because conflict is a normal part of life, I often talk about it. Over the years I've been committed to enabling individuals, groups and worshipping communities to understand and engage with situations of conflict – and I've found this to be fulfilling.

My friends and colleagues will recognize my emphasis on 'different perspectives'. I always seek to acknowledge someone's perspective, even if I can't agree with them; and, when I'm working with people in conflict with each other, I underline the importance of recognizing how things can be seen from different angles, and that our diverse life experiences contribute to shaping the lens through which we see.

We live in a world where there is fear, hurt and destruction because people cannot live with those they see as 'other', whether an individual, group or nation. Therefore, when I'm in conversations about contentious issues in the Church, I'm always keen to talk about the gift the Church has to offer the world if we handle conflict in ways that bear witness to the value of relationship and the flourishing of God's world.

A Theological Reflection:

Genesis 1, Revelation 21 (Creation and re-creation)

A recurring phrase in Genesis 1 is of God creating creatures 'of every kind': the text emphasizes that central to God's creation is a rich diversity. Living in London, I notice this almost daily, whenever I travel on public transport. I overhear other travellers' conversations, but it is striking that most of them are not in English. Instead I hear an array of diverse other languages, spoken by people of many complexions, different from my own. At times this can be bewildering and uncomfortable. And, if we look more broadly, we will notice that tensions over cultural and ethnic differences, and humans' limited capacity to embrace these differences, have been the source of much bloodshed and at the heart of most wars down the generations.

In light of our fractured human history, it seems important to affirm that wide diversity is part of God's creation, and indeed something that God finds 'good'. It is intended to be a source of joy and a cause for celebration, even while we recognize it as an inevitable source of tension and therefore conflict. This is a continual challenge for us in the Church: how to welcome people who are unlike ourselves – who are different. One mark of a healthy church community is its capacity to embrace significant diversity. I wonder how your church measures up.

Jumping to the opposite end of the Bible, the exile John makes this noteworthy comment about the heavenly city that is our future destiny: 'People will bring into it the glory and the honour of the nations' (Rev. 21.26). This seems a significant pointer that the great diversity of God's creation and of human creativity will be fully incorporated into heaven. I believe that heaven is indeed a place of great diversity and difference. It is therefore not a conflict-free zone, but a place where we will bring all our gifts and creativity to addressing our diversity and differences.

Notes

1 Carolyn Schrock-Shenk, 1999, 'Introducing Conflict and Conflict Transformation', in Carolyn Schrock-Shenk and Lawrence Ressler (eds), *Making Peace with Conflict: Practical Skills for Conflict Transformation*, Scottdale, PA: Herald Press, pp. 25–37.

2 Carolyn tells me that she first heard this insight from John Paul Lederach.

3 Samuel Wells, 'The Exasperating Patience of God', Coventry Cathedral, 26 February 2013, p. 8, available at http://www. coventrycathedral.org.uk/wpsite/sermons-talks/.

4 Wells, 'Exasperating Patience', p. 6.

2

Know Thyself – and Value Others

I learnt from my early mentor, Ron Kraybill, that there is really only one place to start in handling conflict better: with oneself. As a trainer, he sought to help people understand themselves better by developing a personal conflict style inventory. He later refined this into a published resource, with the marketing strapline 'Conflict management starts with self-management.'[1] In my years of coaching individual clergy, I have found that greater self-knowledge and understanding of others has been key to unlocking important insights, and to people growing both as human beings and as ministers.

A tool for promoting understanding

There are dozens of different personality profiling tools. Two of the better known are the Myers Briggs Type Indicator (MBTI) and the Enneagram. Every profiling tool has its value. However, each is like putting on a pair of glasses: the tool brings certain things into focus; but other aspects become indistinct and blurred. So, no single tool should be over-relied upon, nor seen as the only way of understanding oneself or others.

For working better with human differences, the *Friendly Style Profile*, developed by Susan Gilmore and Patrick Fraleigh, is a most helpful tool.[2] I learnt about it from Richard Blackburn, director of the Lombard Mennonite Peace Center, and have used it now for over two decades. Let me give you the flavour of it.

In contrast to the MBTI's 16 'types', this scheme is easier to grasp because it is based on just four styles:

KNOW THYSELF – AND VALUE OTHERS

- Accommodating-Harmonizing (linked with the warm colour, yellow).
- Analysing-Preserving (linked with the cool colour, blue).
- Achieving-Directing (linked with the growth colour, green).
- Affiliating-Perfecting (linked with the passionate colour, red).

What do these four styles look like? Imagine a group of four friends in London who decide to take a day trip to Brighton. One of them took the initiative to propose the day, invited the other three – having thought about what combination of people might complement one another – and found a date that would work for them all. He also plans to do the driving. This person has a lot of Achieving-Directing in his profile. A second person has carefully planned their route, worked out what time they need to leave London to avoid the worst of the traffic, and has calculated the costs and what each needs to contribute to cover these equitably. She has also planned when they need to leave Brighton, so that they do not get back too late. Her profile has lots of Analysing-Preserving in it. The third person has organized the car rental, bought the picnic things after finding out everyone's preferences, and packed suntan lotion and a first aid kit. He has also reminded everyone to bring a towel and swimming costume, and their sun hat. This person has a good deal of Affiliating-Perfecting in his profile. The fourth group member has organized some sweets and other snacks, has thought of some games they can play together on the journey and on the beach, and has brought extra money for buying everyone an ice cream. She has also bought some fun T-shirts for the four of them to wear. She has plenty of Accommodating-Harmonizing in her profile. That gives you a little taster of the four styles.

One's *style* is the automatic way that one responds to situations and people. You do not have to think about it: it is how you are wired. (Contrast this, for example, with *skills*, which can be developed, enhanced or lost, depending on whether and how they are used.) The *Friendly Style Profile* affirms that each style has its own particular *strengths*. Whatever your style, certain qualities come naturally, and you readily draw on them as you engage with people and situations. Some strengths of each of the styles are evident from my description. Their combination in our four day-trippers means the expedition has every chance of being a success, with everyone having a good day.

Each style also has 'excesses', which are over-done strengths. When a strength tips over into excess, the impact on oneself or others is negative. This indicates that our vulnerabilities are closely linked to our strengths. Let us revisit the day trip. Imagine that, about half an hour after their departure, the party get stuck in some heavy traffic caused by unexpected roadworks. They crawl slowly forward for half an hour, making little progress. At this point our Achieving-Directing driver loses patience, and decides he is going to do a U-turn and find an alternative route via some back streets. His driving gets more aggressive, and he shoots through a couple of red lights. The Affiliating-Perfecting passenger in the seat next to him explodes, exclaiming that they are all going to die if he carries on like this. The Accommodating-Harmonizing passenger attempts a joke, then says they will all feel better if they have some chocolate; while the Analysing-Preserving passenger has gone steely cold and is scolding the driver for deviating from the tried and trusted route. The day trip is starting to turn into a nightmare, because all four have tipped over into the excesses of their styles.

Managing oneself

A central challenge offered by the profile is to learn how to avoid escalating into the excesses of one's style. Let me illustrate further. My predominant style is Achieving-Directing. Some of my strengths are: being prepared to take the initiative, being ready to accept a challenge and to take risks, and having plenty of ideas and energy. But, if I am not careful, these strengths can tip over into tackling over-ambitious tasks, getting over-extended, and going too fast for others to keep up.

Managing myself means that I have had to learn to say no to interesting projects, when it would mean overloading myself. I have also had to work at slowing down and checking that others are still with me. When I do poorly at managing myself, and get stuck in the excesses of my style, then I can end up getting overwhelmed, losing confidence and becoming paralysed; with other people getting cross with me, feeling that I have let them down or taken advantage of their trust. This is valuable self-understanding – although it is never comfortable facing up to such vulnerabilities.

I experienced a powerful way of using the *Friendly Style Profile* as a trainer on Bridge Builders' week-long foundation courses. Every participant had to complete the questionnaire in advance. Each person then wore a card illustrating their results, which also acted as their name label, during all course sessions. The cards provoked considerable thought. Indeed, reflecting on one's own style, and one's interaction with others of a different style, was often revelatory.

But this did occasionally meet with resistance. One participant was a gifted church leader who had the highest possible score on the Achieving-Directing style. When he considered his potential excesses, he was disturbed: he did not like to hear that this style could sometimes manipulate other people's loyalty, and could be ruthless, and see the end justifying the means. At the close of the course, he took all his notes and belongings with him – but left behind his style card. He had been troubled by the picture that the profile revealed. And with some reason. Many autocrats are probably people who are strongly Achieving-Directing and have never learnt to manage the excesses of their style; but instead have given them free rein, without the benefit of colleagues who could stand up to them. The risk for the embarrassed cleric was that he might not face the challenge of managing himself, and, in his drive to achieve his goals, cause harm and havoc in his dealings with others.

The *Friendly Style Profile* recognizes that most people *change under significant stress*. The profile therefore generates two sets of scores: one for functioning under normal circumstances ('calm'); and another for functioning in more pressured situations ('storm'). For some people the shift from calm to storm is dramatic. I think of one minister, Jane, who when things are calm is strongly Achieving-Directing: she takes the initiative, accepts a challenge, and is a ready source of novel ideas. But when she is stressed, she switches to being Accommodating-Harmonizing: she becomes focused on how others are doing and whether they are happy; she listens carefully to their view point and will sublimate her own preferences for the sake of others. But she stops driving things forward, is more risk-averse, and can be blown off course. This could confuse others, who might wonder whether Jane was two-faced, or just inconsistent. Taking insights from the *Friendly Style Profile*, Jane recognized what was going on within herself; and she learnt to articulate this to others with whom she was ministering. This improved their working relationships. Jane also grasped that, when under pressure, her role as a minister might call for her to maintain impetus and direction, despite her style preference wanting to over-focus on others.

Team building

Working with a style profile can be valuable for a team of co-workers. Once everyone has completed the questionnaire, similarities and differences in results can be explored. The team can be built up by affirming one another's distinctive strengths; and, commenting only on oneself, by enabling individuals honestly to confess their tendencies towards specific excesses. A style profile offers a common, neutral language to explore and talk about the ways we are wired differently, to affirm one another and to be more honest with each other. Such an experience can be eye-opening for a group.

During my curacy in the Church of England, I suggested that our clergy team take a morning to work with the style profile. My training incumbent later cited it as possibly my single most valuable contribution to the team. It helped to highlight some reasons why team members could rub one another up the wrong way. It also demonstrated the value of our diversity: all the styles were covered between us, and each team member could contribute different strengths to the parish's ministry.

A useful team exercise is to explore what is helpful in bringing the best out of someone with a different style from one's own. Imagine someone with a strongly Achieving-Directing style working with a colleague of a mainly Analysing-Preserving style. The Achieving-Directing one will be comfortable with changing plans at short notice and improvising something different. However, for the Analysing-Preserving colleague, this will rarely be a helpful approach: to function at their best, they will need time to think through any proposed significant change to plans. To work well together, the Achieving-Directing person could intentionally choose to slow down: 'Let me check you're with me . . .'; while the Analysing-Preserving person could opt to speak up promptly: 'Hang on . . .' Neither action would come naturally, but each would be demonstrating respect for their colleague's needs. Such challenges face all working with colleagues who are different from themselves – which is normally the case, if we are in a healthy team.

The immense value of diversity within a team is seen when the various strengths of each person's style are drawn on. So, as an Achieving-Directing type, I have benefited from an Analysing-Preserving colleague who helped me avoid rushing into some new projects that would have over-stretched us; while I, with my style strengths, was able to help us be more ambitious and adventurous than my colleague would have chosen without my influence in the team.

Interaction between style and role

One final observation about style concerns the interaction between style and role. While leading Bridge Builders, there was a natural fit between my Achieving-Directing style and my role as head of the service. I did not have to think about whether my style was appropriate to my role. Following ordination in the Church of England, I became a curate in a team of five clergy, of whom I was the most junior. I was also in a defined learning role. Having clarity about my role meant that I had to work at moderating my natural style. I was not there to be in charge, to take the initiative or to set vision and direction, which my natural style would have been happy to do. Instead I had to draw more on my secondary style, the Affiliating-Perfecting, and be supportive of others, look to them to take the lead, encourage them, and be a service-minded team player. Maintaining clarity about my role helped to ensure that I had a happy curacy and got on well with my training incumbent and other colleagues.

Not all curacies or clergy teams are so thriving. Some become so fraught that the relationships break down, and someone ends up leaving. This can happen because colleagues do not appreciate or understand one another's styles. Sometimes those in a more junior or secondary role fail to grasp the nature of their role; or, equally problematic, those in the senior role see no need to release the gifts of a junior colleague. And, when the senior is reluctant to exercise clearly defined leadership because it sits uncomfortably with their natural style, that also creates difficulties.

Knowing oneself, valuing others

Knowing oneself and valuing others who are different: these are basic but essential building blocks for working effectively with people and functioning well as part of a group. If you are someone exercising leadership, then without self-knowledge and understanding of other people you risk leaving a trail of damage and hurt in your wake. I have found the *Friendly Style Profile* to be one valuable tool on the journey to self-understanding and valuing others. Other such tools are available. I think everyone in leadership and Christian ministry should be taking advantage of them. Is there any valid excuse not to do so?

KNOW THYSELF — AND VALUE OTHERS

A conversation with Colin Patterson

Colin was the Assistant Director of Bridge Builders for 12 years, before retiring in 2017. A priest in the Church of England, he previously worked as the adult education adviser in the Diocese of Durham. He is the author of two Grove booklets on conflict.

In what way have you found the idea of personal styles helpful in the journey of knowing yourself?

It's given me a particular type of mirror, I think. Without some understanding of personal styles, I wouldn't have seen that I have my own typical ways of responding to conflict, and I wouldn't be so aware of how they affect other people. By instinct, I'm a conflict avoider. When things are getting tense, I tend to make myself scarce, change the subject, point out what will keep things steady, or put cogent arguments in writing. If the tension doesn't blow over, I easily become a tight-lipped martyr. I'll eventually explode if you push me far enough. Or, as I used to put it, I'm just reasonable and fair-minded! But others might see aloofness and prickliness, a person hard to engage in the conversation that's really needed.

In the *Friendly Style Profile*'s language, I'm prey to some excesses of Analysing-Preserving and Affiliating-Perfecting. Naming this stuff has been a channel for God's grace. And that has gradually changed me. I'm more aware that I've been given a Spirit of power, love and self-control (2 Tim. 1.7), and that I'm not irreversibly locked into negative patterns. I'm more able to imagine alternative ways of responding to conflict. I've developed some better habits. To my surprise, I've learnt to turn my face rather than my back. I'm more aware of the voice inside me that cries out, 'I need you to understand how much this has cost me,' and I can sometimes cut free from it – God's understanding is enough. Another surprise: I've more capacity than I might have guessed for accommodating, harmonizing, achieving and directing.

That person in the mirror has more freedom, more choices.

What has the Friendly Style Profile *unlocked in working with church leaders?*

It's good for helping leaders see some roots of church conflicts. Conflicts can be messy and bruising. Leaders get it in the neck and get stuck. It's hard for them to know where to start, if anything is to get sorted out. I encourage them to focus on *the pattern of relationships* and ask, 'What interplay of personal styles has been happening here?'

Style is very basic. In fact, I find it hard to remember any church conflict where there wasn't a style dimension. It may not always be the biggest factor, but it's often the one that can be most easily recognized and worked with. Look first at styles, not at specific grievances, and there are usually some light-bulb moments: 'Ah, *that's* why those things always bog us down!' The thing is: when you talk in terms of styles, you can shift away from doling out blame. You have a tool for exploring how you can do things differently and avoid getting to this place again. A crucial question is, 'In future, how can we draw on the best of what our various styles can offer?'

It's important for leaders to own their personal excesses. There's a natural tendency to focus on the shortcomings of others, so I make it clear that you don't use someone else's style profile as a weapon against them. If you have a conflict to deal with, the question for you is, 'How is my *own* style part of the mix?' For a while, I was supporting a married couple who were co-leaders of a troubled church. It stayed troubled, but the couple changed! The lifeline for them was that they each started to see why their own style was liable to frustrate the other. 'Colin,' they said afterwards, 'the important thing was that the two of us were able to talk about it together.'

While it's valuable to do style work with a whole team, even when only one member is willing, it's worth doing. A single person behaving less rigidly can get a conflict unstuck. As a one-to-one coach, I encourage review of specific events. 'How were you using what you know about your style profile to lead well?' 'What, if anything, pushed you into the excesses of your style?'

'Is there a familiar pattern here?' 'What will you do next time this happens?' A profiling tool unlocks insights on the impact of concrete actions. It's extraordinary how much hope can be kindled by experimenting with a new behaviour pattern and finding how it changes a relationship. It can be as simple as expressing some gratitude or appreciation first, instead of jumping straight to a contentious point.

What difference can a profiling tool make in helping Christians to value one another?
It helps you to explore why other people are different, without judging them. I reckon there's a bit in most of us that thinks, 'Any normal or sensible person would do things my way, so doing it *that* way is bad.' So, we keep people like *that* at a distance. How to build a bridge? It can be a revelation to have a conversation with somebody rather unlike you and discover why they approach things in such a different way – and why that might have value. If you're a person who speeds up under pressure, speak to someone who slows down – and vice versa. If you get numbed by detail, talk to someone who gets energized by it – or the reverse.

Style instruments are not, however, a magic wand for dealing with prejudice. I remember a training session, in which a group was asked to suggest a biblical character who had an Analysing-Preserving style. 'Judas,' someone offered. It was probably meant as a joke. But I – unlike the person giving the answer – have a lot of Analysing-Preserving in me, and I felt put down. When that style was described, had he only noticed its *excesses*, I wondered?

Clearly, using style profiles doesn't in itself make you value other people. But it helps church groups build on what they already know about developing love and trust. Eating together, sharing stories, talking about unthreatening things – these build rapport. Participants typically share significant personal information and receive affirmation from others. I know stories of transformative moments when every person in a group sincerely said to each other, 'You're a gift to the group because . . .'

But that can end up being a bit fluffy. There's added value in this sort of affirmation: *'Because you have this style,* you are a gift to the group *in these ways*: . . .' You can't say that sort of thing without touching upon specifics. Getting groups talking non-judgementally about actual behaviour gives them tools for dealing with low-level tension. And if you learn how to treat others as valuable when there's only a small conflict, you're better armed to do the same when things get really hot.

A Theological Reflection:

1 Corinthians 12 (Paul's understanding of the body of Christ)

In writing to the early Christians in Corinth, Paul was addressing a group of people whom he had helped to birth as Christians, and whom he had worked hard to teach the Christian way. He knew the group well enough to be familiar with the tensions and conflicts among them. He recognized that one of their biggest struggles was valuing others who were different from themselves: 'I have no need of you'. He also noticed that it was difficult for some to recognize that they had a valuable contribution to make: 'I do not belong to the body'.

What Paul knew, at the deepest level of his being, is that ministry is a team game, and thus that we need one another in building the kingdom. So, in his letter to the Corinthians, he used the metaphor of a body, comprising different organs and senses, to express this. And Paul grasped that we especially need those who are different from ourselves: 'If the whole body were an eye, where would the hearing be?' Furthermore, he understood that those who are strong and in up-front positions also need those who are weaker and less prominent than themselves: thus, he affirms that God gives 'greater honour to the inferior member'. Paul's partnership with Barnabas, Luke, Timothy and others may well have taught him this.

Paul grasped that in the work of ministry, we have different roles to play, among them: pioneer (apostle), proclaimer of God's word (prophet), teacher, administrator, healer and interpreter. No one person can effectively fulfil all these roles. We need different people to play their part. Sometimes the role we are called into will draw upon our style's strengths. Other times we will need to function outside our comfort zone. But in every case, to be effective and faithful ministers of the gospel, we will need to be motivated by charitable love, seeking the health of the body rather than our own glory. There is no more excellent way.

Notes

1 Ron Kraybill, 2005, *Style Matters: The Kraybill Conflict Style Inventory*, Harrisonburg, VA: Riverhouse Press, available from www.riverhouseepress.com.

2 Susan K. Gilmore and Patrick W. Fraleigh, 2004, *The Friendly Style Profile for People at Work*, Eugene, OR: Friendly Press.

3

Grow in Emotional Maturity

I first heard Edwin Friedman, a leadership coach, in the 1990s. 'Only about 80% of what I say is true,' he said. 'But this is true *100% of the time*: the health of any system is down to the maturity and functioning of its head.' Unforgettable, it chimed with what my maternal grandfather had once said: 'If there's conflict in an organization, then look no further than the person in charge: that's where the problem lies.' There's some wisdom here for churches and church bodies. It suggests that everyone in a position of responsibility or leadership within the Church needs to think, 'How do I work at my own growth into maturity?'

Friedman based his ideas on Murray Bowen's *family systems theory*.[1] Working with this theory over the last 20 years has shaped my own thinking about what maturity looks like in human beings. As I now see it, maturity has an essential emotional dimension, and growth comes through slow and sometimes painful work, embracing one's family background.

Bowen proposed that there are *two basic life-forces at play in human relationships*. One is a drive for *togetherness*, that makes us want to be part of a group and desire other people's approval. The other is a drive for *individuality*, that makes us want to be distinct and different from others. These two forces continually pull us in opposing directions. *Self-differentiation*, one of Bowen's most important concepts, is the process by which the forces of individuality and togetherness are managed, a challenge that begins in one's family relationships. When this is handled well, an individual grows up to become distinct from their family; and yet remains fully part of it.

This theory offers a way of picturing maturity. A well-differentiated person, says Bowen, has the consistent capacity to act from their own convictions, beliefs and principles while staying emotionally connected and appropriately responsive to other people. A poorly-differentiated person acts in ways that are highly dependent on, and overly-responsive to other people around them. In its least mature manifestations, a lack of differentiation can result in *emotional fusion*, where one loses all capacity to be distinct from others: one continually runs with the crowd. Or, at the other extreme, it can result in *emotional cut-off*, where one becomes totally distinct from others, losing the capacity to remain emotionally connected to them: one becomes a rebel without a tribe.

Bowen says that fusion and cut-off, though opposite poles, are both an unconscious response to underlying *anxiety*, another key concept in his theory. No one can become fully free of anxiety, so in practice none of us achieves a completely successful balance of togetherness and individuality. However, the good news is that we can all grow in maturity – in our capacity to act in a more self-differentiated way.

Poor self-differentiation, or immaturity, can be seen in two contrasting styles of church leadership. An *authoritarian* or autocratic approach is marked by little listening to others, inflexibility and an insistence on one's own way – signs of emotional distance. Other people feel disempowered and undervalued; they get frustrated, and either give up, or else try to undermine the leader or pierce their armour. By contrast, an *accommodating* or overly-nice approach is marked by attempts to try to please everyone, pleading for everyone to get along together. This tends towards emotional fusion. Other people feel that nothing is properly addressed, that the church is directionless; they get frustrated, and the more assertive or forceful members try to fill the leadership vacuum – or leave in despair. Both styles of leadership are an immature reaction to the challenge of managing one's own anxiety.

As a long-standing tennis fan, I can see this challenge being played out on court. A recent film about the life of Bjorn Borg focused on the 1980 Wimbledon men's final, when he faced John McEnroe.[2] The biggest surprise for me was discovering that, during his early tennis career, Borg had a raging temper which he struggled to control on court. For Borg went down in history as 'the ice-man': master of his emotions, rarely if ever showing them during a match. And this self-control was the key to Borg's extraordinary competitive success. The contrast with John McEnroe, infamous for his temper tantrums, was striking. Who knows how much greater success McEnroe might have enjoyed if he had achieved Borg's self-mastery. I think there's a common pattern at work here. Andy Murray was once known for berating himself and losing his cool on court. But then he hired Ivan Lendl as a coach. The ice-cool, disciplined Lendl helped Murray to manage himself better, reining in his emotional outbursts. This led directly to three grand slam titles. Murray's new-found emotional self-control was the key to fulfilling his gifts and potential as a player.

Each of us has a similar journey to make. Life is full of moments that are rather like missing a vital tennis shot or losing a key point. In our daily interactions with other people, there are times when someone else's behaviour creates an inner surge of anxiety. Most of us then want to reduce or relieve the accompanying discomfort. Bowen's family systems theory suggests that we manage this sort of relational anxiety in ways that we learnt in the family context we were raised in. There are four basic mechanisms we adopt:

1 *Distance oneself emotionally.* This may be expressed physically, for example by taking refuge in a shed, study or other small domain; or it may simply be an emotional disengagement. In its most extreme form, this becomes emotional cut-off, where someone breaks off all contact with the family member who has become the focus of their anxiety. This can be distressing for other family members.
2 *Engage in conflict* – that is, fight. Typically, this goes through a cycle. A pair who are intensely close spark into openly-expressed conflict when something proves difficult, then become temporarily distant; before making up

and getting close again. And the cycle then repeats itself. Things are stormy, but family members know the cycle, and therefore tend not to be too fazed, even though the intensity can be troubling to outsiders.

3 In some partnerships, one partner takes on very little responsibility, thus 'under-functioning', and the other partner takes on lots, thus 'over-functioning'. When the pattern becomes entrenched, the under-functioner may become ill, and apparently incapable of doing many normal tasks; while the over-functioner fills the gaps and does everything. However, this is a reciprocal and largely unconscious arrangement. They both contribute to the dynamic, and neither is more to blame than the other. Sadly, once the pattern becomes chronic and stuck, it is hard to reverse.

4 Parents – most typically led by the mother – focus much of their anxiety on one of their children, who is seen to be especially needy. This 'family projection process' normally results in emotional impairment. In comparison with any siblings, the focus child will have difficulty in coping with the stresses of life and in maturing into an adult who can manage without significant support from others. This pattern is thus often easiest to spot in families with more than one child; but it can be manifest in single-child families as much as in others.

Most families employ a mix of all four approaches to manage anxiety in their relationships, and so cope relatively well with the anxieties of life. But when just one strategy is dominant, the relationship-system becomes noticeably unhealthy and hinders family members from growing into maturity. If you reflect on your own family of origin, you will probably spot which of the patterns is most common. My own family employs emotional distance as the preferred approach. (No one would accuse us of being an overly close family!) And this pattern is one that I can trace cascading down the generations, through my parents from my grandparents and great-grandparents, on both sides.

How does all this bite in Christian ministry? Take the example of David, an Anglican priest who came to see me for work consultancy. He needed support because he had recently taken on the incumbency of a challenging parish, where his predecessor had been found guilty of criminal misconduct. David was struggling to relate to his churchwardens, key lay leaders; he found one of them especially hard to stand up to. I asked him to complete a family genogram – a sort of family tree showing relational dynamics. It became evident, through our subsequent conversation, that he was responding to the problematic (male) churchwarden as he might typically respond to his mother. I encouraged David to see that he could address the difficulties with his churchwarden indirectly, by focusing on his relationship with his mother. He decided to make more regular short visits to his parents. While he was there, he practised standing up to his mother by being clearer about some of his preferences, and not simply accommodating everything she wanted. He did not find it easy. But he made some progress. He then found that he had more courage and capacity to stand up to his churchwardens. He became less anxious in his ministerial work – and enjoyed his whole calling as a priest much more. David was growing in maturity, and it was a delight to observe.

Each of us in the Church, lay and ordained, experiences challenges to act more maturely. There will always be someone who presses our buttons, causing us to respond in the patterned ways we have learnt within our families. If we have eyes to see, we can recognize such a person as a gift sent to us by God, to help promote our growth. Most of us can grow further by examining how we relate to others within our family and addressing an element of the dynamic that we find hard. Sometimes the reverse is also true: addressing a challenge within our church 'family' can give us the strength and courage to revisit things we find difficult within our family of origin.

I want to offer four key principles that follow from family system theory. They provide a framework for mature responses when facing anxiety in our relationships.

1 *Explore being a non-anxious presence.* This does not mean never *feeling* anxious, an impossible target! Rather it is about finding a way to *act* less anxiously, despite the anxiety of others around you. Jesus is a wonderful model of

this. Look, for example, at how he handles himself in the story concerning the woman caught in an act of adultery (John 8.1–11). The religious leaders put Jesus under enormous pressure to condemn the woman. Initially he does not react or rush to respond. Instead he bends down and writes in the dirt. Then, after being bombarded with more intense questioning, he stands and responds. We can guess that he must have been feeling anxious. But he has taken time to think; and he remains relatively calm. After careful consideration, he gives a clear and challenging response: 'He that is without sin among you, let him cast a stone at her.' Jesus does not fall into the blame game. Instead he invites each of those present to take responsibility for their own failings. He is self-controlled, and he is centred: a non-anxious presence. That is not easy. But let us be brave and thoughtful in trying to imitate this aspect of maturity.

2 *Offer and invite clear self-definition.* In other words, be open about what you think and feel. There are good examples throughout church history. Consider the reformer, Martin Luther. In 1521 Emperor Charles V called him to give an account of his controversial writing. He calmly explained why he had written the books piled on the table before him – and why he could not recant their content. Luther is quoted as saying, 'Here I stand, I can do no other.' It is uncertain that he said these words, but they do capture something of his spirit. The point is that he responded to the Emperor not with a defiant protest, but with a reasoned response, giving an answer for the hope that was within him. He was not belligerent – at least on this occasion – but neither was he frightened to say what he believed and why he believed it. This is an example of self-definition for Christian disciples: it is another way of being mature.

3 *Maintain emotional contact when under pressure to disconnect.* Mary of Nazareth, the mother of Jesus, illustrates this principle well. At a wedding – the archetypal family occasion – she looks to her son to address a crisis in the supply of drink. Although he initially dismisses her effort to recruit him, she is not offended, but perseveres. She stays in touch

with her son and with the wedding party (John 2.3–5). But Jesus' subsequent public ministry puts Mary under great emotional pressure. The family's stance becomes that he is mad and needs restraining (Mark 3.19b–34). When they try to take him in hand, shockingly, he appears to distance himself. His brothers eventually gang together to mock his lack of public impact (John 7.2–9). Mary must feel a considerable pull to side with her other children against her firstborn. However, when the governing powers finally bring matters to a head, and sentence Jesus to death, she does not abandon him. She stays next to the gallows, through his final hours of tribulation. She does not look away: she watches her son die an excruciating death; she holds his eye to the bitter end. And, with nearly his dying breath, he responds by carefully entrusting her into the care of a surrogate son (John 19.26–27). We all know that acutely painful experiences typically make us turn away and disconnect. Mary was not typical. She excelled in remaining emotionally connected, despite competing pressures – modelling human maturity.

4 *Seek to stand firm in yourself when the going gets tough.* George Bell, a twentieth-century Anglican bishop, provides a strong example. Bell is best-known for his opposition to the blanket-bombing of German cities during the Second World War. He argued that the fight against the Nazi regime should be conducted in a moral manner without indiscriminately punishing the whole German people for the evils of their government. Bell was heavily criticized by his contemporaries because he would not support the British authorities unequivocally. But he stood firm in his convictions. He did not wilt under pressures to be 'loyal' or 'patriotic' at a time of intense national crisis.

Bell's attitude had deep roots. It grew out of his ministerial approach over the previous 25 years, and out of his understanding of the nature of God's love and purposes. It followed from a long-standing commitment to the work of peace and reconciliation between Christians. And, after the war, Bell went on to make an influential contribution to what became the World Council of Churches – an effort at relationship-building among Christians of diverse different traditions.

However, a post-script is necessary. In recent years, George Bell has been accused of child sexual abuse. After an investigation, the Diocese of Chichester settled a legal civil claim and issued a formal apology. Since then, the Church of England's process in the case has been heavily criticized, and the Archbishop of Canterbury has issued a public apology. It is hard to determine the truth nearly 60 years after Bell's death. Bell may be guilty of the charge. If so, then it shows serious misconduct towards the end of his life. Nevertheless, his other achievements remain worthy of being acknowledged. In relation to his witness and conduct during the Second World War, George Bell provides a striking example of standing firm in oneself when the going gets tough – an under-rated but important aspect of maturity.

Growing into emotional maturity is a road that every Christian – especially every Christian leader – is called to walk, taking inspiration from the great cloud of witnesses who have gone before us. It is not a linear or straightforward progression. It often involves re-engaging with challenging dynamics in one's family of origin, sometimes falling back, before moving for-wards. But the embrace of God is there to hold us, offering us a firm foundation. And, if we are listening, the nudge of the Spirit will always be there, to keep on growing.

A conversation with Liz Holdsworth

Liz was the Director of Mission and Development for the Diocese of Peterborough until early 2019. She has also been a Bridge Builders training partner for the past nine years and has co-trained with me on many occasions.

*What has inspired you to work at self-differentiation and walk
the road to maturity?*

It was a complete revelation to me when, in my mid-forties, I first
encountered family systems theory with its focus on defining
oneself within one's family. The theory helped me understand
the dynamics of the relational network that I'd been part of
throughout my life. I realized that I had choices; and that those
choices could be expressed without distancing myself or cutting
off from others, and without rejecting them. I found that greater
self-differentiation on my part could bring renewal and refresh-
ment into my relationships. It might also bring challenge, as
much for myself as for others – but that's not a bad thing.

It's a lifelong journey to work at growth into maturity. I revisit
my family genogram at regular intervals. I always find that there's
a new insight, and that different relationships come in and out
of focus, as my family's history unfolds. I've noticed that small
steps can have a significant effect, both within my family and in
other relationships. Over the many years I've been working with
the theory, I've become far less anxious as a person.

I've come to appreciate the value of relating to people one-to-
one, and of speaking directly to them, rather than via others in
an unhealthy triangle. Sometimes it's hard to see the patterns
that act against this, because the relationships have been conducted in a certain way for so long. I've become more intentional
about one-to-one conversations, and about making the time for
them. Recently, I've been learning that over-seriousness can be
a sign of anxiety, so that's something I'm chewing over (lightly!).
I've found that humour and paradox can assist in breaking out
of assigned roles: they bring some healthy separation. The greatest danger facing me in my relationships is a tendency towards
fusing with others. So, it can feel lonely, as I work at being well-
defined as a person and a leader.

Edwin Friedman's writing has inspired me: reading *A Failure
of Nerve* for the first time, with its challenging assertions, was
like taking a cold shower – invigorating![3] It's also been invaluable for me to hear about others' efforts to define themselves

in their families or workplace. I've seen what self-differentiation looks like in different contexts, and it's validated the claims that Murray Bowen makes for his theory.

What keys have you found in helping others on their road to growth into maturity?

A first key is inviting people to map out their family genogram and enabling them to ask questions of it in the light of family systems theory. This process can be life-changing. It can be healing and empowering for an individual to have a safe and confidential space, along with a structured process, and to chart the information and insights that emerge. It's also helpful to encourage the person to keep on exploring their genogram and working at their self-differentiation in the family. When they enter this journey, it impacts everything else in their life, including ministry in the Church. That may sound like a grand claim. However, the theory addresses every interaction that we have on an interpersonal level; and such daily interactions are largely what our lives are composed of. You certainly get value for money with this theory!

A second key is to help people explore what self-differentiation means in their setting. The concept isn't easy to get a handle on. Diagrams can unlock understanding for some; for others, it's more useful to give concrete examples of what it can look like in practice. It's also helpful to understand that distancing oneself from others and being fused with another person are both examples of poor differentiation. Neither moves one towards the place of maturity. And it can bring astonishing relief when one finds a way to respect one's own boundaries and those of others, to stay connected, while also handing back anxiety and responsibility to their rightful owners.

A third key is to explore possible barriers to self-differentiation. Fear and anxiety are important ones, speaking through internal voices: 'How will people react if I behave differently?' 'What if I upset other people or provoke a conflict?' Past experiences in one's family and other relationships keep us bound to old ways. The hidden emotional forces within our relationship-systems can leave us feeling as if we have no choices. Seeing and naming these forces can help to strip them of their power. It also helps to attend to the potential 'hostages' within oneself, by asking: 'What do I fear or care about most, that others may use to undermine or seduce me from the path of saying and doing what the situation really requires from me, as a mature leader?'

A common pitfall is to engage in this work with the aim of trying to fix the family or someone within it. Such an effort is doomed to fail and is likely to provoke great resistance. Paradoxically, focusing instead on oneself and one's own maturity turns out to be an unselfish act!

What tips would you offer to others on the journey of growing into maturity?

My top tip is to be aware of anxiety – your own and that of others. Anxiety is central to understanding family systems theory. Spend time familiarizing yourself with your own anxiety. Explore what triggers it, what it feels like, where it comes from, and what your knee-jerk reactions are. Then reflect on how you might manage your anxiety better, especially when experiencing a difficult encounter. Focus on yourself first. Then ponder where the anxiety around you is coming from within the system, and how it may be influencing others' words and actions. Finally, from a calmer position, choose how to respond, in a way that is true to your best rather than your reactive self.

A second tip: don't beat yourself up when you miss a sign and fail to define yourself, or when you don't make your boundaries clear, or when you get caught in an unhealthy triangle. Instead, look to learn from such experiences. There's always an opportunity for this learning because systems and their anxiety are the soup of life in which we wade every day. Continue to look at what's happening in the whole system rather than over-focusing on the presenting symptoms and issues: become more aware of the emotional dynamics. Seek to be 'in the system but not of it' – in the sense of not being driven by its anxieties.

My third tip is to have courage and persistence in seeking to grow, and in defining yourself in healthy, life-giving ways. Resist the temptation to stay in the comfortable place where others define who you are. It's not easy. But there can be a growing sense of liberation. You'll face opposition from those who'd rather you joined their 'herd' and played the game to their tune; but a series of small steps can take you a long way in becoming more fully yourself.

In my experience, being and becoming the person God created you to be really does bring a peace and freedom that the world cannot give.

A Theological Reflection:

Ephesians 4.1–16 (Growing into maturity in Christ)

The reflection at the end of the last chapter noted that the body of Christ needs people to play a variety of roles if the Church is to fulfil its calling. The writer to the Ephesians extends this idea. First, he affirms that the diverse roles are all designed to build up the body of Christ. But then he writes in a new way. The goal, he says, is for us to reach 'maturity' and to attain 'the measure of the full stature of Christ'. Here, then, is what every Christian is called to aim for: maturity, following the example provided by the head of the body.

This is strikingly similar to Edwin Friedman's claim that the health of any system is down to the maturity and functioning of its head. For Christians, this provides a deep reassurance. The body of the Church is assured of healthy growth, thanks to the maturity we find in Jesus. We see it illustrated in the Gospels in diverse ways, under many challenging circumstances. The fact that we do not see that maturity fully evident in the life of our institutional churches may sometimes be depressing. However, this is not because of any failings on Jesus' part. Rather it is down to our collective human immaturity, that of our leaders, and crucially the fallen structures and systems that we have inherited.

The writer to the Ephesians offers a key to our growth into 'him who is the head, into Christ': learning to 'speak the truth in love'. Some have interpreted this as telling people what we think of them, without regard to gentleness or kindness. That misses the intended spirit. Certainly, we should learn the art of difficult conversations and not avoid issues that need to be faced, especially in an overly-nice Church. Some difficult things simply need naming. However, it is equally important to speak the truth of all that is good and needs to be affirmed: so, words of gratitude and encouragement and vulnerability are vital. And when we have grasped both aspects of this truth-speaking, we will find that we can indeed help to 'promote the body's growth in building itself up in love'. That is what will draw us deeper into the maturity of God's life.

Notes

1 Edwin H. Friedman, 1985, *Generation to Generation: Family Process in Church and Synagogue*, New York, NY: Guildford Press.

2 *Borg vs McEnroe*, 2017, directed by Janus Metz Pedersen.

3 Edwin H. Friedman, 2007, *A Failure of Nerve: Leadership in the Age of the Quick Fix*, New York, NY: Seabury Books.

4

Be Real about Power

A bitter lesson about power

An event more than 30 years ago still makes me wince. I was a young civil servant in a section responsible for distributing grants to local authorities. I had been in post for over a year, during which my boss had actively involved me in making decisions, and I had developed some expertise. I had some insight into different local authorities: how effective they each were in using their grants. My boss then moved on. Her replacement, Kevin, soon decided that he wanted to take a different approach. When allocating grants, we would now rely on analysis from a specialist researcher. Effectively, this meant cutting me out of the decision-making.

I was upset at being side-lined. And I was unsure how to raise this with Kevin, who worked in a separate office, and whom I found intimidating. So, I wrote him a memo, one that turned out to be quite strongly worded, reflecting the strength of my feeling. I also copied the memo to the head of our division, because I was worried that Kevin might not listen to me otherwise. The next day, Kevin called me into his office. He was clearly furious. He did not mind that I had raised a concern. What made him angry was that I had copied my memo to his boss, without having first raised the issue with him. He had had an embarrassing conversation with the divisional head earlier that morning, he said, and there were other people of his grade who, put in that position, would have ensured that I *never* got promoted. Thankfully, he added that he had decided not to hold it against me, and to put it down to lack of experience. However, he made clear that I would not get a second chance.

The civil service is a hierarchical organization, with each staff member employed at a certain grade, a certain level of seniority. So, it is clear who has power over whom. Clearly, I had crossed a line by going over Kevin's head, and if I offended in that way again, he had the power to destroy my civil service career. You can be sure that I did not make the same mistake twice! I had learnt to raise grievances directly with the person concerned – and also that it is much better to do so orally first, before committing anything to paper.

A story of the Church and power

The Church is a less hierarchical organization than many, and the nature of power in church relationships is not clear-cut. Nevertheless, power is always at play. I was struck by this during the first major congregational reconciliation process that I led.

The church involved was in a county town and was seen by some as a leading light. The previous senior minister had led the church through a period of astonishing growth: it had more than doubled in size, to several hundred members, over a fairly short period. That minister then left to take up a more prominent appointment. After a gap, in which a preferred candidate turned down the position, a new senior minister was appointed. The church faced several challenges early in his time. For example, an assistant minister, who was much-loved by some in the congregation, was forced to step down by the leadership group; and the decision was taken to close a church-owned business which had been set up during the period of rapid growth but had proved commercially unviable. Tension rose within the congregation, and the senior minister was subjected to a vote of no confidence. He survived, with support from three quarters of the membership. However, the underlying issues and anxiety remained, and so the church invited Bridge Builders to help.

Preliminary research highlighted a range of factors which had contributed to the surge of anxiety within the church. These included some significant losses, both of personnel and projects.

Crucially, there had been little structural reorganization during the period of rapid growth. Most such factors were well outside the control of the current senior minister, who (it seemed clear to me) was being unfairly blamed for a range of systemic issues within the church. However, this was not a message that some in the congregation wanted to hear. As the reconciliation process progressed, it became evident that there was a group of influential people determined to see the senior minister leave, and they pushed hard to bring this about. Among the most vocal was a family whose children had special needs, who felt that they had not received the same level of pastoral support from the current minister as they had previously. This was symptomatic of the failure to establish an effective congregation-wide pastoral ministry in a church of that size. However, the family's hurt carried a powerful emotional force, especially given their long history in the congregation; and others were swayed by their heavy criticism of the minister.

The senior minister stayed the course through the demanding reconciliation process. However, he wisely concluded that the scale of opposition from influential people was going to hamper his capacity for effective ministry. And so, a few months after the process concluded, he found another position. He left wounded, and it took some while for his confidence to be rebuilt.

I could not forget this church's story. Etched in my own mind was the reality of power struggles within the life of a church. Since then, I have seen several cases where a 'scapegoat' – often an ordained minister – is blamed for a whole range of losses and problems facing a church. Every minister has weaknesses and shortcomings; but scapegoating blows them out of all proportion.

Getting the subject out in the open

Christians can be reluctant to talk about power in the life of the Church. This may derive from naivety, embarrassment or simply blindness. It can be hard for them to believe that fellow believers might use their influence inappropriately, and there are surprisingly few books written on the subject. But no one with responsibility in the Church should be under any illusions: power is always at play and is only safe if it is named and acknowledged.

Here are some general maxims that I think Christians are wise to accept:[1]

- *Power exists, and we all have power.* Simply to be alive is to embody and exercise some form of power. Does that seem surprising? A former colleague used to talk about 'the power of the baby': as someone without children, he was struck by the power of even a very young child to influence their parents.

- *Power lies not just in the individual, but also in relationships.* Power can come from personal attributes, such as articulacy, strength and beauty, or from one's position, which may include conferred authority. However, these forms of power can only be exercised in relationship to other people. Imagine a head of government stranded alone on a desert island: most of their power would be lost. Or a church example: a person arriving as a new minister has some positional power but is not yet known and trusted. Compare long-standing members of the congregation: they may not occupy formal positions within the church's structure, but they carry powerful influence *due to their relationships and history within the body.* Crossing those people unnecessarily, or early in ministry in that church, is likely to prove costly.

- *Power is fluid and difficult to measure.* Power is easier to recognize than to define, easier to sense than to pin down. And it can seem to slip away for no obvious reason. Ministers sometimes bemoan their sense of powerlessness, and they typically underestimate the significant power that they carry. For, in many people's minds, they act as God's representatives. And, like everyone else, they have power that is inherent or ascribed (for example, from gender, class and race) and power that is achieved or attained (for instance,

38

from education, marital status and role). But those things often seem invisible and are rarely named.

- *Power itself is neither positive nor negative.* Power simply exists and can be used either for good or for ill. So, Christians do well to reflect upon their own power and how they are using it. Does the term 'a powerful person' have a good or a bad ring for you?
- *Denying one's power is a small step away from abusing it.* It is vital for clergy, in particular, to recognize their *own* sources of power. This came home to me while conducting research into a church that had begun in the 1970s. I interviewed all the previous and current pastors. One was a man who had then gone on to teach at a local seminary. He had recently been dismissed from his post because he had engaged in a series of adulterous relationships with seminary students over several years. It also emerged that, when he was a congregational pastor, he had begun a sexual relationship with one of his parishioners. (The damage wreaked by these revelations was extensive within the wider community and among several families and congregations.) I noticed what an articulate and charismatic man he was. His interview was the longest that I conducted, because he kept talking in such a compelling way. He made this striking comment: 'No one told me that I was a powerful person until I was found to have abused that power.' How revealing: if he had been more self-aware, he might have handled himself better.

The history of child sexual abuse in the Church is a salutary reminder that significant power inequities can become occasions for wrongdoing. A relatively small number of clergy have used their power – some conferred by their priestly or pastoral position – to take advantage of children and other vulnerable people. Such action is immensely destructive, as the testimonies of survivors have helped to highlight.[2] It also tarnishes the reputation of all clergy, and reduces trust in the priestly or ministerial office, detracting from the many faithful clergy who use their power for the common good, to build up the individuals and communities that they serve.

Using power well

Stories of abuse highlight how vital it is for all in Christian ministry to be aware of their own power. At the very least, Christian ministers need to acknowledge their power to themselves and to those with whom they regularly reflect on their ministry. Working as a coach with clergy, I encourage them to focus first on networks of relationships and then on themselves: 'Where does power lie in this system?' 'How are you looking to use your own power?' These two questions can help a minister to move from feeling stuck to finding some clarity about next steps.

This brings us back to the positive aspect of power. For power is 'the ability to get things done or to influence outcomes'.[3] Without power, none of us – ordained or lay – can be effective ministers of the gospel. We need power to make a difference. And faithful ministry usually involves finding ways to empower others, helping them to use their own gifts appropriately to serve others and to build up the kingdom of God.

Let us, therefore, give power good press too. Sometimes there is an unhelpful distinction in Christians' minds between God's power, seen as good and legitimate, and human power, seen as bad, always tarnished by sin. It is more fruitful to understand power both in terms of its origins in God and in terms of human capacity – and to recognize that the Holy Spirit can work as much through human agency and exercise of power, as through purely divine means.

Systemic power

Power works in human societies in ways that go beyond individuals and their relationships. There are systemic forces, centuries-old, that lead to structural inequalities in the distribution of power. Then individuals internalize societal patterns of domination. So, in British society it can be hard to break free when you belong to a group that has historically been oppressed, such as women or those from minority ethnic communities. But hope is provided by those who resist being defined by a particular identity, and find ways to exercise power, despite intense opposition and discouragement. This is why the witness of historical figures has been so inspirational. Think of examples such as Emmeline Pankhurst and Millicent Fawcett, leaders in the movement for women's suffrage in the UK; Rosa Parks and Martin Luther King, leaders in the US civil rights movement; and Nelson Mandela and Helen Suzman, leaders in the struggle against apartheid in South Africa. Each of these figures defied the limitations that others wanted to put upon them, and stood up and spoke up for what they believed in. Critically, they also mobilized others and took collective action, recognizing that only a social movement could overturn historic forces of oppression, and establish more just and equitable distributions of power. They each had a dream; and they were prepared to lay down their lives for it.

Systemic power-imbalances are as present within the Church as they are in society. Indeed, the Church tends to reflect wider society much more than is often recognized. I was struck by this when I began training for ministry in the Church of England. I was part of a cohort of around 175 ordinands at a college in London. I was surprised, even shocked, to notice that the number of ordinands from an ethnic minority could be counted on the fingers of two hands. Given that most of the ordinands came from churches in London, where there is a huge ethnic mix, there was clearly something wrong. It suggested that those with responsibility for encouraging and discerning priestly vocations were blind to the potential of some members of their congregations; and that those members struggled to imagine themselves as leaders within the Church of England – possibly because of a dearth of role-models.

All this points to a level of – probably unconscious – racial prejudice within the structures of the Church of England. Many would be reluctant to admit it, since it is contrary to the gospel that the Church seeks to embody. It is hard to notice when a *system* denies that all are equally valued in the eyes of God. But, again, it reflects wider British society. For example, in 2017 nearly two thirds of the main boards of Britain's biggest companies had no ethnic minority presence at all. Yet around

14% of the whole population is from an ethnic minority; and the proportion is higher in London, where most major companies have their headquarters.

Addressing structural power-imbalances, whether within society or the Church, is not a straightforward matter. But a useful starting point is to help people see with new eyes. I have therefore been encouraged to see some Church of England initiatives seeking to train clergy and lay leaders to be more aware of their unconscious bias. This is one sign that some are taking the issue seriously.

Responding personally

What would it look like for each of us to reflect more deeply on ourselves in relation to power? Here are some questions to ponder:

- What are my own sources of power, and how can I be less embarrassed about these?
- How can I use my power to serve the common good and build up the body of Christ?
- What unhealthy temptations do I face in the use of my own power?
- In what ways can I encourage others to use their power for building God's kingdom?

The apostle Paul wrestled with how to use his power appropriately. As a young man he had been violent, crushing what he saw as contrary to God's law. After his conversion, he was persuasive, seeking to convince people of the new revelation of God in Jesus Christ, while avoiding violence. Near the end of his life he wrote this: 'God did not give us a spirit of cowardice, but rather a spirit of power and of love and of self-discipline' (2 Tim. 1.7). This captures a right use of power. We each face our own journey in God's service. But without discerning how to use our power, we will be much less faithful and effective than we are called to be.

A conversation with Rosemarie Davidson-Gotobed

Rosemarie is the Church of England's National Minority Ethnic Vocations Officer, and the founder of the annual Sam Sharpe Lectures. Raised in a Baptist church in south London, she was the Baptist Union's first Racial Justice Coordinator. She attended an early week-long training course with Bridge Builders.

What has been your experience of encountering power dynamics in the life of the Church?

I am female and of African Caribbean heritage, and this has shaped my experience. I often engage with people who say they want to see greater diversity and inclusivity of people of colour in the various roles of responsibility within the Church. However, I then find that they often struggle with their own sense of discomfort as to what that might mean both for themselves individually and for their group. While certainly not true for everyone that I have worked with, I notice that resistance and obstruction keep occurring. I also recognize that the patterns I encounter were established long before I was on the scene. And, if I'm honest, they show little sign of disappearing any time soon.

I don't want to suggest that power is always used negatively in the Church. On the positive side, I've had a friend or ally use their powers of association and information to get me into places and spaces that would otherwise be closed to me. For example, by making a strategic personal introduction or using their influence to create a platform for me.

Nevertheless, as a woman of colour, I find that those holding greater power in the Church may assume that I am from a disadvantaged background and that my perceived historical heritage is inferior to that of the prevailing white heritage. It's not unusual for those in more powerful roles, often men, to emphasize their position over me in small – but subtly aggressive – ways. Typically, this comes with a smile. However, the tone used is designed to put me firmly in my place, or to act as a shot across the bow. Further, I've sometimes experienced those above me trying to confine the parameters that I work within. When this happens, I sense that there is a concern not to discomfort the comfortable or to challenge the status quo too directly.

A central way in which I find prejudice being perpetuated is when the Church acknowledges racism as a sin that needs to be confronted, yet at the same time no one in the Church is ready to own up to a racist attitude. How can this add up? The Church has often talked about being delighted and blessed by people of a Black, Asian and Minority Ethnic (BAME) heritage, and even of valuing our contribution. However, I'm left rather puzzled. I know that what we value, we treasure and take care of. We also pass on that sense of value in the stories that we tell, to avoid it getting lost. Yet, after nearly 30 years of working in cross-cultural understanding and racism awareness, I find myself repeatedly facing the same themes, histories and issues that I encountered at the start of my career.

What would you offer as ways of being more empowered as a Christian disciple, especially if you come from a minority group within a society?
My first encouragement to is to remember not to absorb the overt and covert negativity that comes with being identified as a 'minority'. I've found this to be a subtle yet powerful mechanism to reduce and restrict us. What our British society describes as an 'ethnic minority' is part of a world majority where Christianity is vast, growing and dynamic, albeit facing its own challenges. I think that being more empowered means not apologizing for the much-needed gifts that you bring to the table of church life in this country.

Second, I'd urge you to familiarize yourself with the history of BAME people who were here before your family arrived in this country, and to do so using your critical faculties. This narrative is a crucial part of the journey that brought many peoples here to make a home for themselves and their children. I've found that this story holds rich veins of experience, along with resources of needed information and helpful support.

It sounds obvious, but in a society where often you are regarded as 'other', don't be surprised if you find the same attitudes reflected in your local church. If you anticipate this possibility, you'll be less discouraged when you encounter such attitudes.

How do you see the Church working better at engaging with issues around ethnic diversity in her midst?

I am thinking here mostly about the Church of England because that's the context in which I'm now working, although similar challenges face other denominations in the UK. The Committee for Minority Ethnic Anglican Concerns, known as CMEAC, has already developed several initiatives and resources for use within the Church of England to help her become more effective and inclusive. I'd like to see more intentional applications of that significant body of work, which can be found on the Church of England's website.

My observation is that church systems run the danger of not moving beyond 'tick box' exercises, and that they tend to only focus on what can be measured. For some, there seems little appetite for delving beneath the surface to reach the roots of our current lack of inclusion, presumably because doing so has had a painful history. To my mind, there needs to be a significant cultural reconstruction before we will see the Church of England being more inclusive. I recognize that such change takes time, but we've had an ethnically diverse society in England for at least 70 years. How much more time do we need?

In my view, it's not enough to encourage more people of BAME heritage to come forward to train for ordination. I think it's also important to understand why they are Anglican, and why they would want to remain within the Anglican fold. This is especially important for people of BAME heritage who were born and raised in the UK because there is so much that we do not know about these church members. Most of the Church of England's current BAME leadership were born outside the UK and they bring a different perspective, which sometimes does not reflect the experiences of those born and raised within the UK more recently.

One final observation. Theological colleges could make an enormous impact by requiring students to explore theologies from around the world, and by having required reading lists that are diverse and inclusive. This could help to prepare culturally-competent clergy, as they are exposed to new thinking. I look forward to that day, when all these issues around ethnic diversity and inclusion will be self-evident and part of the cultural norm.

A Theological Reflection:

Matthew 26.57–68 (Jesus on trial before the High Priest)

The Dutch painter Gerrit van Honthorst painted a masterly depiction of a snapshot from this scene in Matthew's Gospel. It is one of the treasures of the National Gallery's collection.[4] In the painting, we see Jesus being accused by the High Priest Caiaphas. Where does power lie? It appears to lie with Caiaphas, the man in the seat of power, with the book of authority before him. In front of him stands a bedraggled man, in the dock. Does he stand defiantly? Or belligerently? Van Honthorst depicts Jesus as a gentle, lamb-like man, looking directly at his accuser, but in a resigned, even pained manner. He is not cowed, but neither is he resisting. He is a sacrificial lamb knowing that he is going to the slaughter.

If we believe that God is fully present in Jesus, then what do we think is going on here? Why is Jesus silent before all the accusations against him? If he is God's anointed one, why is he not defending himself, and putting Caiaphas and the others right? Why does Jesus remain so quiet and accepting of what is going on? Why does he not call on the angels and archangels to defend him? Why does he not call down fire from heaven, like the prophet Elijah? Why does he not *do* something?

This story offers a window into God's use of power. We may expect or long for God to use power in a dramatic way to achieve desired ends. There are times when we would all like to see a bit more divine intervention to address the problems of the world.

Jesus demonstrates that God's use of power is different from what we might like. Instead of using force, God's power is seen through Jesus' laying down of his life for others, bearing all the unjust accusations and indeed the sin and violence of the whole world. Caiaphas and his ilk fail to understand this, not grasping what God's power is really like. The New Testament writers invite us to see and ponder God's use of power in a new way: not as something to be exploited or imposed, but as something that is used sacrificially in the service of others.

Notes

1 I have drawn upon: George B. Thompson (ed.), 2005, *Alligators in the Swamp: Power, Ministry and Leadership*, Cleveland, OH: Pilgrim Press; and Carolyn Schrock-Shenk, 'Power and Conflict', in Carolyn Schrock-Shenk (ed.), 2004, *Mediation and Facilitation Training Manual: Foundations and Skills for Constructive Conflict Transformation*, Akron, PA: Mennonite Conciliation Service, pp. 78–9.

2 See https://www.iicsa.org.uk/. The inquiry covers England and Wales.

3 Don Freeman, Lancaster Theological Seminary, quoted in Schrock-Shenk, 'Power and Conflict', p. 78.

4 See https://www.nationalgallery.org.uk/paintings/gerrit-van-honthorst-christ-before-the-high-priest.

5

Use Good Theory

I wonder if your eyes glazed over when you read the word 'theory'. Bear with me! In this chapter I want to argue that theoretical models can help us to pay attention to what we might otherwise miss – a bit like using the right lenses. Conflicts can be complex, and we need to look for underlying patterns and invisible forces if we are to understand them properly.

A model of social conflict

It was 1996, and I was sitting in a class on international peace-building at Eastern Mennonite University. The teacher, John Paul Lederach, was talking about the conflict in Northern Ireland. Since I had visited there only a couple of weeks before, I was all ears.

Lederach summarized some formative events, as follows. In 1921 a border was created, separating the six counties of Northern Ireland from the other 26 that then formed the Republic of Ireland. The majority Protestant community, fearing a loss of identity and the creation of an all-Ireland and Catholic Republic, took action to retain control. Roman Catholics and Irish nationalists experienced discrimination in securing jobs and in the allocation of public housing, the gerrymandering of electoral boundaries to prevent nationalists getting elected, and oppressive security measures. The predominant aim on the Protestant side was to ensure that Northern Ireland remained part of the United Kingdom and was not ceded to the Republic of Ireland.

48

Now Lederach sketched out a diagram on the board. It was a model of the progression of conflict, derived from Quaker peacemaker Adam Curle. This highlighted three things: the relative power balance, the awareness of the conflict, and the move from conflictual to more peaceful relations. (See Figure 5.1.)[1] This model, Lederach indicated, could help us understand the more recent conflict in Northern Ireland. It had begun (stage 1) with people trying to raise awareness of social injustices. Then it progressed in the 1960s (stage 2) to a more proactive campaigning by civil rights groups. This was overtaken by a shift to a more violent phase dominated by both republican and unionist paramilitary groups – an ongoing feature of the tensions until the 1998 Good Friday Belfast agreement. However, by 1990 it was also clear that a further shift had begun (stage 3): a move into direct negotiations over securing a peaceful settlement. But, Lederach noted, there was nothing inevitable about progress forward to a more peaceful place. The incidents of paramilitary violence in the 1990s, despite peace negotiations being under way, showed that the conflict could cycle back to an earlier stage.

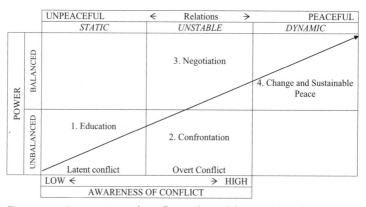

Figure 5.1: Progression of conflict (adapted from Lederach, 1997).

I left that classroom excited: I had seen how useful a theoretical model could be in charting and explaining the progression of a complex social conflict. The diagram stuck with me.

Curle's model is not neutral: there are social justice values built in. He believes that where parties are in conflict, one should strive for a better balance of power, and a more equal and just relationship between them. Otherwise there will not be a sustainable peace.

This is illustrated well by the history of the movement for women's suffrage in Britain.[2] In 1832 the Reform Act set the stage for conflict, by explicitly ruling out women from voting. The first wave of opposition concentrated on education and awareness-raising (Curle's stage 1) because so many were blind to the injustice of the situation. This lasted throughout the middle of the nineteenth century, during a period when further parliamentary reforms extended the vote to more men.

Forty years after the first Reform Act, a national society and a national union were formed to campaign for votes for women. This moved the conflict to Curle's second stage: open confrontation. Suffragists now sought a new act of parliament. But by the start of the twentieth century, despite widespread support, they had failed to achieve a change in the law. Men in power resisted the change; and the ensuing frustration engendered a more militant campaign. This was established via a new union, led by Emmeline Pankhurst and her daughters. These women promoted direct action, which included shouting down speakers, hunger strikes, window-smashing, and the bombing of unoccupied churches. This represented an intensification of confrontation.

The outbreak of the First World War in 1914 led to a hiatus in political life, including the suspension of the militant suffragette campaigns. However, during the war many women took on roles previously undertaken by men, which helped to create a defining shift in public opinion. Then, as the war was concluding, the conflict moved into Curle's third stage, negotiation. In 1918, the coalition government passed legislation that enfranchised all men over 21, as well as all women over 30 who met certain property qualifications. It was an important step forward. However, the conflict was not concluded for another ten years when, in 1928, parliament finally granted the vote to women on equal terms with men. Curle's goal had been reached: a sustainable peace.

I find Curle's approach helpful for a number of reasons:

- He emphasizes that conflict is usually a matter of power differentials.
- He advocates building a stronger interdependent relationship between disputing parties, with greater recognition of each other's needs.
- He is realistic: peace is not inevitable and there can be regression to earlier stages of the conflict.

Implicit in Curle's model is the idea that at each stage different players may come to the fore. For example, advocates and campaigners are needed at Stage 2, while negotiators and peacemakers are needed at Stage 3. The two sets of skills and approaches do not necessarily sit easily together, and it is rare for one person to combine both. But it can happen. In Northern Ireland, Ian Paisley and Martin McGuinness were both acclaimed because they made a major personal transition in the roles they played, in the years after the Belfast Good Friday agreement. They were able to start working together: against the odds, they shared political leadership of Northern Ireland. Such a shift in role is not easy, nor is it necessarily welcomed by those in the leaders' respective camps.

The nested theory of conflict

John Paul Lederach also introduced me to a model developed by Máire Dugan.[3] It acts as a useful complement to Curle's work, when one is trying to decide where best to focus effort as a bridge-builder.

How to intervene? That was the question facing Dugan when she was working on a case of violent conflict. It had arisen between two rival gangs of boys in a North American high school, one a group of black boys, and the other white. Dugan reflected on the different approaches that might be taken. A *conflict resolution practitioner*, she thought, would focus on the *presenting issue that had given rise to the violence*, in this case the wearing of the Confederate flag by the white gang members. The way forward would be to *promote dialogue*, talking about the significance of the flag, and also about the relationships within which this had become an issue. On the other hand, a *peace researcher* would see the situation in the context of a society built on racial and economic inequality and oppression; and would focus on *the systemic problem underlying the violence*: racism.

Each approach, Dugan recognized, would have its limitations. Conflict resolution might help to reduce tensions and repair broken relationships, but it would not address the racism. A researcher's analysis could focus attention on the bigger picture but would not address the immediate crisis and relational breakdown. Dugan discerned that the two approaches could be *integrated* by focusing her efforts on the high school, not just on the two gangs within it. A *peace-builder*, she suggested, would seek both to address the specific issues and relationships and to address the systemic racial problem; for example, by introducing training on diversity and race awareness across the whole school.

To generalize this insight, Dugan proposed a *nested model* of conflict (See Figure 5.2.)[4] It recognizes that social systems are like layers of an onion; and it highlights the value of action taken at the *sub-system level*. This means a level between society as a whole, and the people directly involved in a concrete dispute. In Dugan's example, the high school was the appropriate sub-system.

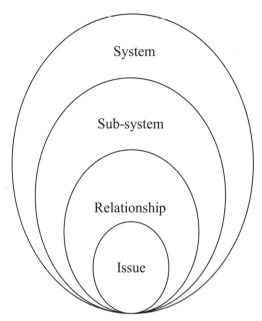

Figure 5.2: A nested theory of conflict (based on Dugan, 1996).

I have applied Dugan's model fruitfully in coaching clergy who are wrestling with a situation of conflict. Tina, an Anglican priest, came to see me because she was struggling with her role as a trustee of a charity, a task that came with being incumbent of the parish. She was not happy with the way the charity was being run. The main problem, she said, was the chair of trustees, whom she found disrespectful and dismissive. She was feeling stuck, and unsure how to address the tension. I listened to Tina as she shared her understandable frustrations. After a pause, I suggested that she take a large sheet of paper and draw the board-room table, identifying all the trustees, in their usual seats. Then I invited her to map the principal connections between the various people, using different coloured pens.

This mapping exercise was revealing. It showed that Tina was not, as she felt, completely isolated on the board: there was another trustee with whom she connected well, and who was supportive. He did not come to every meeting. But when he came, he could be relied on to speak up affirmatively if she raised a concern that was not shared by the chair – especially if it was a view that the chair might otherwise dismiss. The diagram also highlighted a powerful trio of men: the chair, the secretary and the administrator. They worked in concert and sought to dictate how the charity was run. The only other woman on the board had been selected by the chair, possibly to give an illusion of gender diversity. She rarely spoke at the meetings and was not prepared to rock the boat. So, Tina was not hopeful that building bridges with her, and developing some female solidarity, would help in addressing Tina's concerns about the charity. However, she could now see that it was worth nurturing her relationship with the one trustee whom she found supportive. She therefore now planned to meet up with him for a chat over coffee, outside board meetings. And she wanted to encourage him to attend the meetings more regularly. This would strengthen her aim of ensuring that the charity focused better on its charitable objects, rather than just advancing the chair's pet projects.

As I worked with Tina, I had Dugan's model in mind. Tina had come focusing on a presenting issue – the chair's disrespectful behaviour – and was uncertain how to proceed in her relationship with him. As she talked, I sensed that there were some systemic issues at play, including a misogynistic culture within the charity. I also guessed that this reflected something of the wider societal culture within which the charity was located. Like racism, sexism is not an easy structural problem to grapple with; however, Dugan's model prompted me to invite Tina to reflect on the charity, a key sub-system, and to explore the interactions and connections between trustees. Although this did not directly solve any problem, it opened up greater awareness of the bigger picture and offered a new avenue to explore. Tina then felt more empowered. At a subsequent session we explored how she could be less reactive to the chair's treatment of her. We considered how she could handle herself better in response to his provocations.

This enabled her to be less anxious (see Chapter 3) and gave her a way of addressing the presenting issue that she had come with.

Seeing beyond the immediate

Conflicts – including church conflicts – usually need something more than a sticking plaster. Theoretical models of conflict can help us to pause, probe and persevere. Curle's model teaches us that conflicts typically need to go through a stage of intensification and confrontation before entering a stage of negotiation and discernment about how to address the problems or injustices. The voicing of complaints and conflict is therefore not something to be ignored, but something to move towards and to explore. Lederach's application of the model reminds us that forward progress is rarely linear: things can cycle back to an earlier stage, while Dugan's model teaches not to over-focus on presenting issues and strained relationships, otherwise we may miss attending to the larger systemic issues that are contributing to the tensions. The most fruitful way to engage with systemic issues is through working with a sub-system in which they are manifest.

It turns out that there is nothing so practical as good theory.

A conversation with Lia Shimada

Lia is a freelance trainer and consultant on diversity. She specializes in mediation, community facilitation, conflict coaching and participatory research. Lia has previously worked on implementing the national strategy for diversity and inclusion for the Methodist Church in Britain, and on peacebuilding in Northern Ireland.

What do you see as the main benefits or limitations of theoretical models in engaging with conflict in the life of the Church?
It makes my heart sink when a church leader, in desperation, says, 'Give me some tools!' The world of mediation and conflict resolution is awash with tools of different shapes and sizes. A tool, though, is only as good as a person's understanding of how to use it.

At their best, theoretical models can be a gift to the Church. They can aid clarity in understanding, provide a common vocabulary, and reveal a sense of order within the chaos. For clergy and lay leaders facing a clamouring conflict, the act of engaging with a model might provide confidence to take the first step into the fray.

Yet we are wise if we sit lightly to our models – gleaning what is good and letting go of what might hinder. How does a particular model touch us, and draw us closer to compassion? How does it stimulate us intellectually? And how does it help us – or not – to be rooted in the lived work of bridge-building? Such questions can help our discernment. Above all, we would be wise to remember that no model, no matter how well-designed, can fully express the presence of God at work in the conflict, and in us.

Sometimes the best way to use a theoretical model is to consider its limitations rather than its utility. Take a classic model introduced on many mediation skills training courses. This seeks to illustrate the relationship between the positions that people take and their underlying concerns and more fundamental needs, in this way. (See Figure 5.3.)

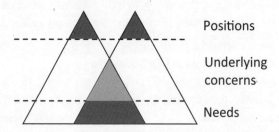

Figure 5.3: Positions, concerns, needs.

On one level, the logic underpinning this model is fine: it helps us appreciate that the position a person takes is 'just the tip of the iceberg'. Shoring this up is the bulk lying below the surface: a hulking mass of deeper concerns and needs just waiting to fell a relationship, or a community. To resolve a conflict, says this model, all you need to do is to help the parties identify their shared concerns and needs. See the neat over-lapping triangle! Here lies common ground: once we find it, we'll find a place where things will be 'happy ever after'.

When I'm teaching mediation, I include this model in my course. Then I ask the group, 'What's wrong with this picture?' Occasionally, someone alights on the answer immediately. More often, it takes time to find our way there. Critically, this model assumes that the icebergs are equal in size and, therefore, in power. To mediate with wisdom and integrity, though, is to understand that the distribution of power is rarely – perhaps never – equal. To proceed on an unchallenged assumption of equality is not only ignorant; it can also be dangerous. What we learn from challenging a model in this way is theory that serves us well as mediators.

For me, the concepts developed through 'narrative mediation' offer a helpful antidote to the model of equal icebergs. (I'm thinking of Monk and Winslade's approach.)[5] At its heart, this approach helps us to understand how stories shape – and can re-shape – a conflict. It takes seriously the recognition that people are diverse, their identities fluid and multiple, and that power is slippery. When freed from the pressure to find common ground, and from the fiction that we're playing with equal power, we can work with new honesty with the stories that people carry into conflict. In doing so, we can generate new stories – which can become building blocks for a bridge across the divide.

Can you illustrate how you've applied a narrative model in working with a conflict?
I once accepted a commission to facilitate mediation of a conflict that straddled two different world views. A few years previously, a church with a majority African and Caribbean congregation had started a small outreach project to provide hospitality to vulnerable people living in the local area. While committed, they were also a small and ageing congregation, and soon reached their limits. Then a group of young activists joined as volunteers. They were different in being mostly white, middle-class, educated and atheist. Initially, it seemed like a brilliant collaboration: the congregation housed the project, and the young volunteers brought time, enthusiasm and idealism. But before long, cracks appeared

along several fault lines: Christian – atheist; old – young; black –
white; politically conservative – politically progressive. Poor
communication and missed signals exacerbated the tensions.
Differing opinions over the church building were the presenting
focus, but underpinning this were larger questions: What is the
purpose of 'church'? Should a sanctuary always be a sanctuary,
or can it double as a bicycle repair workshop? Whose supplies
take precedence: the project's or the Sunday School's? And
what does this say about a church's ministry priorities?

By the time I got involved, the crisis had moved beyond breaking point. The young activists had wrested the project away from
the church and were running it through a community centre. The
congregation felt dismayed and betrayed. I was asked to bring
the two groups of volunteers together for one final conversation,
to say a 'good good-bye'. An important question was this: what
narrative would be told about the project?

Following individual meetings with all the participants, we
gathered on a Saturday morning for a joint conversation. From
the outside, it appeared that the young activists held the upper
hand; they'd gained control of the project and were now running it independently. The balance of power, though, was more
nuanced than first appeared.

Over two hours, both groups shared their perspectives on how
initial hope and enthusiasm had descended into frustration and
animosity. As the mediator, I helped them to work intensively
with their stories, grappling with differences in interpretation.
We sought to speak openly about diverse cultural experiences
of the project and the conflict. Every now and then, we found
moments when the narratives intersected or held the promise
of a more spacious dialogue. That gave energy to generate new
stories of shared endeavour. Crucial was acknowledging regret,
on all sides, and identifying murky areas needing clarity.

Through the conversation, the church volunteers articulated
their fear that the congregation would be 'written out' of the project's story. As they talked, the young activists realized that although
they'd carried on using the original name of the project – an African

word for hospitality – they didn't understand its origin. Here, at a crossroad of realization, the church volunteers gifted the story of the name to the young activists. From there, a new story unfurled that linked past, present and future.

The mediation didn't 'resolve' the conflict by turning the clock back: the project remained firmly in the stewardship of the young activists, at a new venue. However, from the encounter emerged a much-needed recalibration of relationship, and a rebalancing of power. By gifting the story of the name to the young activists, the church volunteers rewrote their church back into the story. The young activists – now custodians of a project that had taken flight thanks to the vision and dedication of all – agreed that this was the story that they would tell, from then on.

A Theological Reflection:

Acts 6.1–11 (Conflict in the early church)

In Acts 6, we have the first recorded church-wide conflict in the young Jerusalem church. It comes during a period of rapid growth. We note that this church was composed of two distinct groups: Hebrew- and Greek-speakers. All Jews; but speaking a different mother-tongue. Such linguistic and cultural differences can contribute to misunderstanding and tension, as they did then. The conflict is latent, until it emerges that some of the Greek-speaking widows are being neglected in the daily distribution of food. Then the Greek-speakers start to mobilize, and they voice their complaint against the Hebrew-speakers: the conflict becomes overt and confrontational. As Jews, they would have known that questions around justice for widows were questions about the community's faithfulness to God's covenant. That was why it mattered so much. Adam Curle's model invites us to explore how the conflict progressed, noticing power differentials and choices made about empowering others. Máire Dugan's model suggests looking at how a systemic injustice can be addressed within a sub-system.

How do those in church leadership respond? We can surmise that they were feeling under pressure because of the major church expansion. The pressure would have been compounded by the accusations of injustice and unfaithfulness. Let us note some things that they did not do. They did not get reactive and defensive. They did not just tell others what to do – or tell them to simply go away and pray about it. Instead, recognizing that the issues mattered deeply, they called the community together to discern how to proceed. When conflict comes, the temptation is to separate into camps and to avoid the other side. The Apostles resisted that temptation. They had the courage to face the challenge and the feelings of hurt and injustice among the Greek-speakers. They took the conflict towards negotiation. This meant listening deeply to one another.

We can infer that it emerged during this dialogue that feeding the Greek-speaking widows was not the only issue. There was also a question about the make-up of the leadership group. It seems that all the existing leaders were drawn from among the Hebrew-speakers. When the Apostles offered a way forward, they proposed expanding the leadership group to include some able administrators. However, judging from their Greek names, it seems that all the newly selected leaders were from among the Greek-speakers. The Apostles figured out that it was not just a question of expanding the size of the leadership: there was a question of representation within the leadership that needed rectifying. Addressing that deeper issue took them towards a more sustainable peace – at least for a time.

It seems the Apostles initially envisaged the additional leaders in a limited role, focused on distributing aid. However, after the Apostles had laid hands on them and commissioned them, the new leaders went on to exercise a full apostolic ministry (Luke's narrative focuses on the witness of Stephen and Philip). Perhaps most significantly, this church conflict contributes to the early Christians' understanding of God's purpose in drawing people into the kingdom of God. For this early conflict is in many ways a preface to the later, and bigger, church-wide conflict that culminates in Acts 15. There, the issues are not just between Jews who speak different languages, but between Jew and Gentile, two irreconcilable groups for most Jews.[6] Notice, therefore, how conflict in the Church can be the arena for discerning God's will for the Church and the world; it can bring to light hidden things that need attention; and it can open a fresh understanding of God's mission and God's welcome of all peoples into the heavenly kingdom.

Notes

1 Table slightly adapted from: John Paul Lederach, 1997, *Building Peace: Sustainable Reconciliation in Divided Societies*, Washington, DC: USIP, p. 65; Lederach in turn adapted this from: Adam Curle, 1971, *Making Peace*, London: Tavistock.

2 I have simplified the events for the sake of clarity.

3 Lederach, 1997, *Building Peace*, pp. 55–7.

4 Máire Dugan, 'A Nested Theory of Conflict', *A Leadership Journal: Women in Leadership*, Volume 1 (July 1996).

5 Gerald G. Monk and John Winslade, 2000, *Narrative Mediation: A New Approach to Conflict Resolution*, San Francisco, CA: Jossey-Bass.

6 However, judging from Paul's letters, it seems that the conflict rumbled on for many years and was not as neatly resolved as Luke's account in Acts might suggest.

6

Shepherd the Process

In the Introduction, I told my story of entering the bridge-building field through a short mediation skills course. Before that, I had often felt stuck when facing conflict situations. Part of the excitement was discovering that one could navigate a way through. Resolution could be found through a simple, well-structured process. Bridge Builders adopted a mediation model learnt from Ron Kraybill and other Mennonite trainers, for use in British church settings. What does this process look like? A case study provides the best way to illustrate, simplified for presentation here.

A case of three couples

The case involved a group made up of three married couples: Simon and Natalie, in their early thirties, and two older couples, in their fifties. Age was therefore one of the power differentials. The three men, commissioned as 'elders', formed the leadership of an independent evangelical church. The tensions were precipitated by the sudden resignation of one elder. A range of concerns then surfaced, which had previously been latent. Collectively the men agreed that they needed external help to address their conflict. Hence, an approach to Bridge Builders.

I was called by Simon, the church's pastor and the youngest elder, who explained the background. He added that while elders' wives were not formally part of the leadership, in practice they were as involved as their husbands; and key tensions revolved around the wives' interactions. The mediation sessions clearly needed to include them, not just the men. This meant having three marriages in the room, along with the dynamics between the six individuals. And . . . one of the older couples' marriages was in crisis.

Preliminary work

I proposed some pre-mediation work to help everyone to reflect on themselves and get to know one another better. We would begin by exploring the strengths and excesses of their respective styles, using the *Friendly Style Profile* (see Chapter 2). Such preliminary work plays a useful role in starting to de-escalate tensions, making for an easier entry into the mediation process. Simon and the group accepted the proposal.

When the profile results were received, in advance, one pattern stuck out: the three women had strong scores for task-oriented styles, while two of the men had much higher scores for people-oriented styles. This suggested that the wives were significant in getting things done in the church – hence the importance of including them in the mediation.

At our first gathering, my co-mediator and I presented an overview of the profile's four styles, helping the participants to make sense of their scores. Then, focusing on each person in turn, we invited the other group members to affirm the strengths of the focus person's predominant style. So, for example, the group said that Simon was flexible and quick to forgive and forget; while they affirmed that his wife, Natalie, was meticulous and good at paying attention to detail. We ended up with a list of a dozen or so strengths for each person, recorded on the chart. Receiving such direct feedback is relatively rare. Typically, it proves remarkably encouraging for individuals to be affirmed in this way. It proved so here, with the emotional temperature dropping down a notch, as the session progressed.

I then invited the participants to reflect individually on the potential excesses of their styles, and to acknowledge two or three that hit home. We went around the circle, this time each one only speaking about self. Simon acknowledged that he could sometimes be over-flexible in his approach to deadlines;

while Natalie recognized that, at times, she could see things in black and white terms. Each one made their own confession. This step helped everyone to reflect self-critically on how their own style could have a negative impact on others. Such self-reflection is a vital step in people recognizing and taking responsibility for their contribution to tensions among them.

The mediation process

Our next session began the mediation process proper. My co-mediator was Jane, a member of Bridge Builders' network. We opened with some introductory elements, setting a welcoming tone. It helped that Jane and I had already built trust with the participants through the preliminary session: they were less tense overall. However, tension is always high at the start of a mediation. This places a priority on the mediators to manage their own anxieties and to adopt a calm presence.

Jane and I outlined the main steps lying ahead: hearing an initial account from each person; a framing of the central issues to be addressed; then, working on those issues one at a time, by building understanding and developing agreements for the future. We clarified that we were not there to judge right or wrong, nor to tell them how to resolve things. Rather, our role was to structure their conversation, and to assist them in discerning their own way forward. We invited them to commit to listening carefully to one another, avoiding interruptions, and speaking only for themselves. Then I entrusted our time to God with a spoken prayer.

Next, we asked each participant in turn to explain their principal concerns; and either Jane or I then summarized. With six people, this took a while. But it was vital that everyone had an equal chance to share some of what they were carrying. A break followed, for Jane and me to distil the key issues. We identified the following:

- the resignation of one of the men from the eldership and its impact on others;

- how the two older women worked together on church activities;
- the roles and responsibilities held by the three wives;
- Simon and Natalie's joint ministry together; and,
- how they would all relate together in future.

We checked, and there was agreement that this list covered what they needed to talk through.

We began by exploring the resignation. The man concerned explained what had led to his decision. He did not find this easy and needed support from the mediators to keep going. He concluded by expressing regret at the suddenness of his action. After commending his openness, we invited others to talk about the impact on them. They sought to try to understand each other's perspective. Helpfully, Simon and the remaining elder expressed regret for their part in things not being well handled: such admissions are often key to building a bridge towards reconciliation. They also expressed their sadness at losing the man from the eldership; and said how they missed his gifts. I was impressed by everyone's honesty, and by their ability to take responsibility for themselves and to extend grace to one another. Jane and I then drew the session to a close.

At our next gathering, the participants addressed more of the issues and, with the mediators' help, reached constructive agreements on ways forward. Some were small steps: for example, the two older women agreed to have a regular coffee together as part of rebuilding trust. Actions like these can be significant in relationship-building and are not to be undervalued. What mattered here was that the participants were committed to taking these steps.

Our final session was delayed by two months. When we gathered again, Simon and Natalie's joint ministry was the top outstanding issue. Natalie had raised this at the outset; so, we began by hearing from her. She talked about the way the church leadership team was formed when she and Simon first arrived. Natalie had understood that she would be part of the leadership group, albeit not an elder, because of an earlier precedent. She expressed how hurtful she had found it, after her arrival, when the two older men then dismissed the possibility: it was painful that they could not see her making a leadership contribution. Natalie found it costly to talk about what had happened: she was close to tears. The two older men responded well: they recognized that they had not handled the situation sensitively; and expressed their regret for the hurt it had caused her. Natalie also apologized for having subsequently withdrawn from church involvement for a year, nursing her hurt. As before, we could feel bridges being built, given the openness and honesty with which each person spoke, without blaming others – albeit with emotional intensity. (Such a low level of blame and attack is rare.)

After a silent pause, I asked the older couples whether they might want to offer Natalie some affirmation. All four responded by expressing heartfelt appreciation for Natalie's gifts and their pleasure at seeing her involved in church life recently. This was helpful. However, looking at Natalie, something deeper was needed: I had a strong intuition that the group needed to lay hands on her, and to pray for her. This was not something I had tried before during a formal mediation session. But I risked proposing it. Critically, when I checked with Natalie, she affirmed her welcome of this step. So the others each gently laid a hand on Natalie, and several of us prayed. Then her tears flowed. By the time we had finished praying, Natalie's demeanour had changed: it was as if a huge weight had been lifted from her, and she could stand tall again.

We concluded by exploring how the six of them would relate together in the future, as individuals, as couples and as a group. They agreed a sensible way forward, given the limitations of the situation; and they recognized the importance of implementing what they had committed to, in maintaining healthy relationships with one another.

Later, each participant completed an evaluation form. Natalie supplemented this with a letter to me and Jane, which we treasured. She said, 'I appreciate so much how you cut through and focused the discussion in our group . . . You brought light into what was a particularly tricky and complicated situation.' These words picture beautifully a gift that mediators can bring to a conflict. Those involved often feel stuck amidst a jumble of confused events, hurt and pain. They cannot see a way forward. But mediators, by framing the central issues neutrally and providing a structure to explore those honestly and constructively, can offer participants a way to engage with difficult topics and emotions, to come to terms with the past, and to make commitments for the future.

Natalie offered a personal reflection on the final session: 'Thank you for going with your hunch and inviting the group to pray for me and lay hands on me. I hadn't been ministered to for a long time; and felt emotionally heavy. During the prayer time, I felt a real releasing. I felt affirmed by others and ultimately by God.' At its best, a mediation process can unlock this: a releasing of emotional burdens, and a new connectedness with other people and with God. Such lovely transformations, although not common, happen often enough to be a source of rejoicing.

Looking back

In a recent conversation with Natalie and Simon, I asked what had stuck with them, looking back on the events of a dozen years previously. Natalie was grateful that she had maintained her relationship with the other two couples, despite the difficulties they had journeyed through. She continued, 'I still recall the significant pain of that time; but I also remember the great healing we experienced through the mediation sessions.' With welling emotion, she recalled the group's prayers for her: 'That time of prayer was hugely healing for me, spiritually and emotionally.'

Simon noted that the conflict had occurred early in his ordained ministry: he was just two years out of theological college. It was a fragile time for him. He said, 'Finding a way to get over the hump of that difficult conflict gave me the confidence to continue in ministry.' He had learnt how hard we sometimes need to work to overcome misunderstandings with one another.

Both mentioned how the mediation process taught them the value of checking understanding – of ensuring that what they had heard was what another person wanted to communicate. I was encouraged to learn what a long-lasting positive impact the mediation process had made. Simon summed it up by saying, 'We both discovered a new sense of God's heart for reconciliation.'

Lessons for ministry

Few people will ever need to participate in a formal mediation process to address a relational conflict. Fewer will be called to train as mediators to lead such a process. However, there are insights from mediation that can be applied to everyday church ministry, whenever tension arises:

1 *Focus on providing a process to explore the tension.* See yourself as a shepherd of the process. Set aside any determination to secure your preferred outcome; instead, assist those involved to discover a way forward together. Although harder when you are a party to the conflict, you can still advocate for good process. A classic trap is to over-focus on the *content* of a fractious issue. Pay more attention to *the way* the discussion happens, by attending to the process.

2 *Dig below the surface to unearth the deeper, underlying concerns.* For example, at a clergy staff meeting one upset colleague might complain, 'I haven't heard anything positive from you about my planning of that service: you've only been critical of things you didn't like.' If you ask a question about why this matters to the individual, you might hear, 'After all the hard work that I put into organizing the service, I need to hear some words of appreciation before we start reviewing what might've been done better. Otherwise I'll be discouraged from making such effort in future.' This gets to the underlying concern, the need for some affirmation; and opens up options to

address that concern. Without such exploration, the opening statement risks only being heard as a pointed finger, increasing the tension.

3 *Recognize people's deepest human needs, underlying their concerns.* One feature of our case study was how much each person needed to feel they had been listened to. This is a fundamental human need: to be heard and understood. So, when tensions arise, provide space for everyone to speak; and show that you have understood. These are vital steps to finding resolution and a way forward. Equally important, we each need to be valued as a person, as Natalie found. Each of us needs to know we are appreciated. Such valuing can be shown in a host of ways. A good start is to create space for words of appreciation to be offered, without pretending there is no room for growth or improvement.

4 *Develop your skill set*, including those employed by mediators. A key skill is listening deeply, and then checking understanding. You can do this by offering a summary of what you have understood. Just as useful, to elicit deeper sharing, is asking an open-ended question or inviting someone to say more. You could say, 'Help me understand why this matters to you.' Or, 'Tell me how this has affected you.' These indicate your commitment to listening, and invite sharing at a deeper level.

5 *Avoid trying to fix the situation.* Focus, instead, on promoting people's understanding and recognition of one another. Such a focus is maintained by being a faith-full shepherd of the process.

A conversation with Joanna Williams

Jo is a Baptist minister and Director for Reconciliation at the Blackley Centre in Elland, West Yorkshire, helping people to transform conflict and make peace. An experienced community and church mediator, Jo has been a training partner with Bridge Builders for many years, co-leading on their 'mediating interpersonal conflicts' course.

What first drew you into the field of mediation? Why have you stuck with it?

I have an abiding childhood memory: seeing my mother standing in our kitchen, crying in my father's arms. Her anguish was caused by a devastating conflict within our church. Feeling powerless to change things, she had watched my grandparents being badly hurt by others. I remember clearly our family's bewilderment at how people in a loving Christian community could behave in such destructive, hurtful ways.

I've long desired to find alternative ways to deal with our tensions. When a tutor at a Baptist college, I attended a mediation skills course with Bridge Builders. It was an 'ah-ha' moment: my learning made sense and connected with who I was and what I believed. It proved the start of my ongoing journey of serving in mediation and reconciliation work.

I have seen how mediation can transform immense pain and heartache; and create improved relationships and positive outcomes. The empowering nature of mediation appeals to me. People are not managed, nor are problems solved for them – instead a mediation process enables people to find their own way through their difficulties, while creating space for real understanding. This can transform the present, and the future: they can learn new skills for handling difference and tension.

I've also seen how people can grow in knowledge and understanding of others and of themselves. We're increasingly encouraged to see certain people in our world as 'other': as less worthwhile, valid or human than ourselves. Mediation offers a corrective, a way of changing perspective: through the process, all find themselves equally valued and heard. (A reminder that we're all beloved children of God, who delights in each one of us.) An opportunity is created to see our 'opponent' differently, to listen and understand them, to work with them to effect change. That's what a good mediation process offers.

It also offers space to redress hurts, to find or extend forgiveness, and effectively to shift problematic relational dynamics. There's a sense of sacred space in the mediation encounter that can surprise and inspire, as God's Spirit works through a simple process, effecting transformation.

As a mediator, what keys would you point to in being a shepherd of the process?

Mediation enables people to have the conversations that they need to have. So, we're facilitating to reduce misunderstanding, and to create 'safe space' for difficult issues to be explored in constructive ways. Crucial is ensuring real listening. Too often, we think we're listening when we've only heard a fraction of what's been said: our mind has wandered off, busy constructing our response.

Providing a summary is therefore a vital feature. When used by mediators, summaries slow down heated conversations, provide clarity, prevent misunderstanding, and help people feel that they've been heard. Summarizing is more effective, however, when offered by the people themselves. They usually need to be coached, as it's not something people do naturally. When someone offers a careful, accurate summary of the other, it can prove a pivotal moment in their conflict. New understandings emerge, opening a gateway to expressions of regret, once people recognize the impact of their behaviours.

This happened once in a mediated group conversation between a minister and some church 'elders'. There'd been conflict in their church, including serious and hurtful allegations about the minister's conduct, breakdowns in communication, and different individuals trying to assume control. During the intervention process the minister had, patiently and graciously, engaged in several difficult interpersonal mediations. A recurring theme was people misunderstanding one another. Overall, I was impressed by how they worked together during the process: significant progress was made. This conversation was due to be the concluding session.

It began well, and several issues were identified and positively addressed – when the minister suddenly offered a personal comment. Her reflection was well-meant but unfortunately phrased, seeming judgemental and inflammatory. There was a horrified silence, and I could see all the good work of previous months disappearing. Rather than letting others react, I summarized what she'd said. When she heard my summary, the minister was visibly appalled: that was not what she had meant at all! She was astounded when I suggested that this was what others might have heard. It illustrated how misunderstanding can arise from poorly chosen words.

We looked at how she could've expressed herself differently. She made another attempt. This time, I asked one of the elders to summarize. We repeated this several times, until there was a full understanding. One elder then expressed regret for his part in the conflict, recognizing that it was based on misunderstanding. Tears were shed, sadness and regret were voiced, and we paused the process: for prayer – and for hugs! We then had a fruitful conversation about communication, including how easy it is to misunderstand, and the need to find ways of checking and clarifying meaning. This conversation proved to be their turning point.

It seems simplistic to say that one timely summary can change a situation from a destructive to a constructive one; but it's been key on many occasions. Hence, when training mediators, I say, 'If in doubt, summarize!'

What advice would you offer to church leaders about attempting to mediate a dispute?
It's important to control your need to solve the problem. Church leaders get involved in resolving conflicts because others look to them to 'put it right'. Once you take on such a role and allow your opinions, judgements or feelings to be brought into the mix, you've taken over – and risk becoming part of the problem. Instead, remain impartial, build rapport with all parties, listen carefully, and enable listening between others. If such impartiality isn't possible, then look for someone to mediate with you – or instead of you.

Have the structure of the process you want to follow written out in front of you. Then stick to it! Create space for listening; identify common ground and issues of disagreement; work through each issue in turn; build an agreement. Trust the process, and make it work. Remember, this isn't about you.

Maintain as calm a manner as possible, controlling your own anxiety – the parties will be anxious enough! Don't be surprised if things get heated or uncomfortable: they wouldn't be there if they were getting on well. Gradually reduce the heat by calmly running the process. People will get stressed or behave inappropriately. Therefore, at the outset, lay out ground rules of respectful listening and careful speaking, to which you can return later.

Take time – this isn't a quick fix. Prepare carefully. Ask yourself: what's *really* concerning them? People feel overwhelmed by conflict and intense feelings. Therefore, a calm, well-managed process can be a life-line, offering a way through. Identify the deeper concerns behind people's positions. Help them address their real needs, beyond perceived goals. In doing so, you'll be offering them hope, and the opportunity to begin a journey towards reconciliation.

A Theological Reflection:

Luke 24.13–35 (The walk to Emmaus)

I love Luke's beautifully crafted story of the disciples on the road to Emmaus, for it encapsulates the gospel in miniature form. Two disciples are walking to their home in a village outside Jerusalem. They are trying to come to terms with the painful events of the previous few days, in which they have seen their beloved teacher humiliated and executed, and their hopes dashed. Another traveller falls into step alongside them. We note that this is God's way: to draw alongside us in the midst of our pain and confusion on life's journey. Even if, like the two disciples, we may fail to recognize the form in which God comes to us.

The traveller then asks the couple what they are talking about: he is committed to listening. They are bemused that he does not appear to know what has recently happened in Jerusalem. He asks a brief question that elicits the whole story: 'What things?' Of course, the traveller already knows what has happened. However, he knows how important telling the story is for those who have lived it. He does not try to short-circuit their need to process and make sense of what has happened.

The disciples pour out their account of recent events, telling of their deep disappointment at what befell Jesus. The traveller listens, without curtailing their story. But once he has heard them out, the conversation takes an unexpected turn. The traveller begins to instruct them, helping them see the events in a new light, informed by a fresh reading of their scriptures. Still the couple do not recognize him. Given the late hour, they persuade the traveller to let them host him for supper. It is then, 'in the breaking of the bread', that they finally recognize their beloved Lord. The Italian painter Caravaggio depicts this moment of recognition in his stunning painting of the meal at Emmaus. He portrays it as a shocking surprise for the two disciples.[1]

There can be unexpected surprises for each of us when we face into and process a conflictual experience. We can learn uncomfortable things about ourselves, discovering that we may have been foolish or made a misjudgement. We may discover that, against our expectations, God is made known amidst the pain and suffering. We may need to revisit our reading of Scripture. In a eucharistic meal we might also find a new closeness to the brokenness of God. And we will hopefully discover afresh the reality of Jesus' resurrection, and find that we have a new story to tell that is worth sharing with others. That was the journey those Emmaus disciples went on, accompanied by Jesus. As we face into conflict, that can be our journey too.

Note

1 See https://www.nationalgallery.org.uk/paintings/michelangelo-merisi-da-caravaggio-the-supper-at-emmaus.

7

Make Space for Feelings, Silence and Touch

When there is a conflict, one temptation is to over-focus on what the dispute is about. We imagine that if we sort out 'the issue', the content of the fight, that will resolve the matter. But it is equally important to deal with the emotional territory. In this chapter I suggest that exploring how people *feel* about what is going on is as important as the content. I consider how space is needed for *silence*. Then, I reflect on the place of *touch*.

A family story

How good are you at expressing your feelings? How does this compare with others in your family? You will have noticed that members of the same family differ in how well they express their emotions. In some families, it is the women who are comfortable expressing their feelings, with the men emotionally reticent. In one family, the reverse was true. The father and son were both quick to articulate their feelings. One might say, 'I find myself getting angry when car drivers don't respect cyclists on the road and leave no space when over-taking. My blood begins to boil.' Or the other might say, 'I feel dispirited when you blame me for the difficulties in our relationship: it seems unfair to suggest you don't play a part.' In contrast, the mother and daughter both struggled to express their feelings verbally, especially when there were tensions.

One day the father came back from a course with a hand-out that offered two sets of words. The first group were for articulating positive feelings: words you might use when your needs or desires have been met. On this list, were: cheerful, thankful, contented, interested and hopeful. Broadly, this was the 'happy' group. The second set covered more difficult feelings arising when needs or desires are not met. They included: disappointed, worried, annoyed, mixed-up and embarrassed. This was the darker group, which could also express anger and shock. After discussion, the parents pinned the sheet up on the wall near their dining table. A couple of days later, the moment arrived. They were talking over supper. The father asked the daughter what she felt about something awkward that had happened at school. The girl was silent. After a pause, the mother asked, 'Can you point to a word on the list that expresses your feeling?' The daughter looked at the sheet and eventually pointed to a word. The father said, 'So you felt embarrassed when your friend did that?' The daughter nodded assent. It was a positive development: the rest of the family now understood the impact of what had happened.

This little family story points to a wider truth: articulating the emotional dimension can be vital in giving others a deeper insight into the significance of an experience.

A falling-out between ministers

The senior and associate minister of a large urban church – Rob and Ben, respectively – had worked together well for several years and were friends. Then, in an unguarded moment, Rob said something to Ben that upset him and strained the trust between them. That incident led to a fracture in their relationship: they became more distant. However, they kept working together, and did not tell their lay leaders about the rift. Instead they continued ministering, but with a background unease between them. Over the following years, things ticked along – until a new incident suddenly brought tensions to a head. Given the level of intensity, they recognized they needed external assistance in working things through. That was when they approached Bridge Builders.

I mediated alongside a colleague. After hearing the story of Rob and Ben working alongside one another, we explored the most recent trigger. Rob gave his account: he had learnt that his associate, Ben, had sought to raise doubts about whether Rob should continue as senior minister, and to garner support for his view among the lay leaders. We then heard a different account from Ben. However, it did not seem as if we were touching the guts of the incident. I invited Rob to talk about the *emotional impact*. How had he felt when he first heard the report? 'I felt as if Ben had stabbed me in the back.' I suggested that this was a view of what Ben had done, rather than an expression of how it had left him feeling. Rob tried again: 'I felt betrayed when I heard that Ben had been lobbying against me.' We were getting closer; but I suggested that 'betrayed' was still an interpretation of Ben's action, rather than an expression of Rob's feelings. How was he left feeling? Concerned? Angry? 'I was distraught when I heard that Ben had been speaking against me among the lay leaders. I was shocked that he'd seek to undermine me, after so many years working together.' Suddenly the dynamic shifted. Rather than feeling accused, Ben now could grasp Rob's upset. To consolidate this, the mediators invited Ben to summarize what he had heard. He offered a fair summary of what Rob had felt and how he had been affected. And Rob agreed that Ben had grasped it. We had travelled to a new place: the two pastors were now sharing at a deeper level. Later in the conversation, we followed a similar process regarding the incident that had painfully affected Ben years previously; and Rob was able to show that he understood the emotional impact for Ben. This provided some important reciprocity.

Exploring the emotional dimension unlocked a less defensive, more fruitful conversation between Rob and Ben over four mediation sessions. Due to the distance that had developed between them, there was a long list of issues they needed to discuss. On these, they reached some concrete and specific agreements. However, we sensed that they had not really rebuilt a deep level of trust. At our final meeting they both said that they could not now envisage continuing to minister together, beyond the short term. Rob also concluded that it was time for him to move on to another post.

This might not look like a 'successful' outcome. However, the two pastors ended their mediated conversation with a deeper mutual respect, greater understanding, and absence of bitterness and recriminations. This had not seemed achievable at the outset. The key had proved to be speaking about the emotional impact of past events; and finding a way to do so that avoided blame, and enabled speaking from the depths of the heart.

Helping to articulate feelings

How might we do better at giving space for people to articulate their feelings? Imagine you are chairing a meeting or facilitating a group. When something crops up that has been difficult for a participant, you might smooth over it. Or, more helpfully, you could move towards it, asking, 'How were you affected by that?' or, 'How did that leave you feeling?' You will then be demonstrating your appreciation that the emotional impact is as significant as the event. It will be clear that you welcome people being more vulnerable. Even if you are simply a group member, you can still ask, 'I wonder how that impacted you?' or, 'I wonder what that felt like for you?' Providing the chair allows the space, you will be helping people to explore their emotional landscape. (Note that, sometimes, a question about emotional impact is better raised in private, especially when there is a low level of trust within the group.)

There is a wider question of how to extend *corporate* emotional vocabulary. You are best able to propose this as a facilitator or chair of the group, and you need to be sensitive. Take soundings from participants before making a proposal. Otherwise you may trigger a surprising emotional reaction! If there is support for this type of growth, various resources are available online. You could do worse that post a list of feeling words on the wall of your gathering place.

A place for silence and touch

Sometimes simply finding the words to express feelings can unlock a stuck situation. Other times, something else is needed. I recall an incident in a small team leading a training course. During a team briefing, we were reflecting on a personal account that one of the trainers had given, to illustrate how we can be imprisoned by our childhood reading of a relationship. But, the trainer had suggested, when we are brave enough to explore that reading with the relative concerned we may discover that they have a more liberating interpretation than we had ever realized. He spoke of his father: 'Talking with him about a defining time in our relationship unlocked a new openness and love during the closing year of his life.'

Although calm and composed when telling the story the previous day, my co-trainer was suddenly overcome with emotion as we reflected on its impact. Seeing the surfacing feelings, one team member was quick to respond: 'Shall we pray for you?' The emotional colleague could not speak. Another team member simply reached out her hand, and gently rested it on our colleague's arm. She said nothing; just looked at him with quiet compassion. This was what our tearful colleague most needed – not words, simply the reassurance that we were with him, and would remain present in the depths of what he was feeling. He slowly calmed down, regaining his composure.

Here was something realized intuitively and expressed via silence and touch. Let us explore both these expressions further.

At ease with silence

Being comfortable with silence is a gift in working with people amidst their tensions and intense emotions. It is a sign that we are not frightened of the deep places in a person's life. When we are comfortable with silence, the person we are alongside will know it is safe to reveal the pain or confusion lurking in the depths; knowing we will not rush to smooth things over or sort them out. Instead, we will sit, tenderly allowing them to bring difficult thoughts and feelings into the light; and leaving them to find their own way in exploring them. This may include struggling to find the words to express difficult feelings. How to become more comfortable with silence? There is no easy answer. One way is simply to practise silence, especially corporately. There is scope for us to integrate intentional silence better into our church meetings. One group I am part of does so. Our practice evolved because the group includes people of different faiths and none. After touching base, we begin with five minutes of silence, ended by the sound of a gentle bell. This helps us to be gathered and focused once we start our meeting's business. Church councils and committees can benefit from such a practice, ended by a spoken prayer. Extended silence can also helpfully be used after a long contentious discussion, when a group has struggled to discern a common mind – helping a group to regain composure and centredness on God.

Many find silence difficult to befriend. I have found two approaches helpful. One is taking a retreat where much of your time is in silence. A residential religious community can be the ideal location. A second approach is to engage in regular contemplative prayer or meditation. This can be done at home in your normal place of prayer; on a walk outside; or in a church building, with others, or alone. (For some, like parents of young children, creativity is needed to identify a suitable space, and to carve out space to enjoy it.) See silence as 'a gateway to God', says David Runcorn.[1] He affirms that it is about placing yourself before God, and recognizing that God is at the centre of life, rather than yourself. Embracing this reality strengthens us to be more comfortable being silent with others, amidst the depths of their life's struggles.

Appropriate touch

In Chapter 6, we heard how some mediation participants were invited to pray for Natalie. Two elements were significant for

MAKE SPACE FOR FEELINGS, SILENCE AND TOUCH

her. One was the words of blessing that the others prayed. But equally significant was the gentle laying on of their hands. Touch made words of care and blessing incarnate.

At St Martin-in-the-Fields, the church offers prayer for healing immediately after the main Sunday morning service. On one occasion, while working there, I went forward for prayer myself. I was feeling somewhat at sea over a challenge facing me; and was concerned about my relationship with a family member. I knelt at the altar rail, and a lay team member came up to pray for me.

After hearing my account, this elderly lady rested one hand gently on my shoulder; and held one of my hands lightly cupped in hers. She then prayed. The prayer was somewhat long-winded, and her words washed over me, without being particularly helpful. However, what stayed with me was the deep impression of being cradled by God. This was conveyed by the lady's gentle touch: it left a powerful sense of God's loving care for me. At the close, this was consolidated when she anointed my forehead with oil. I had experienced the healing power of touch.

Touch can be powerful as a sign of how close God is to us, and how tender God's care is for us. Touch can speak to us of God's love, more eloquently than any words.

How do we incorporate touch into ministering to those facing conflict? With care! It is usually too risky to incorporate the laying on of hands in a formal conciliation process, when tension is acute and escalated. Perhaps it is better for touch to be integrated into the everyday ministry of the Church. Obviously one option is regularly to offer prayer for healing, with the laying on of hands. Another is to teach people exercising pastoral care, lay and ordained, to integrate touch into their ministry. Those from the charismatic traditions will be familiar with this and know its value; there is no reason for others of different traditions not to share in the practice. Some training will prove helpful, as touch can be uncomfortable or problematic. A key guideline is that it needs the other person's permission. For it to be beneficial, it also usually needs to be done lightly and gently.

If practices like these are a normal part of the life of the Church, those travelling through conflict can be encouraged to seek her ministry along their journey towards reconciliation.

A matter of the heart

What do exploring feelings, drawing on silence and employing touch have in common? All are diverse ways of reaching the heart and moving beyond the head. In seeking to transform conflict, I have found that engaging the heart can overcome blocks on the road to reconciliation. Exploring feelings takes us to a place of human connection that can unlock empathy and understanding. Holding silent space allows hidden internal work to happen. Touch provides the reassurance that a person is not alone. Together, these three gifts help us open pathways to peace.

A conversation with Frank White

Frank is a retired English bishop. He was the Bishop of Brixworth and then the Assistant Bishop of Newcastle, in the Church of England. Frank participated in the second week-long Bridge Builders course in 1997, becoming a long-standing supporter of the organization.

What drew you to engage with transforming conflict in the life of the Church?
The honest answer is *necessity*. I'd been appointed as an archdeacon and quickly recognized that this ancient office carried regular exposure to conflicts and disputes in churches. Some of these had smouldered on for years. Thankfully I already knew the Mennonites and their work in peacemaking. I was soon at the Mennonite Centre in London for a week-long conflict resolution course. This gave me both a wider theological understanding of conflict and tools to help engage with people for whom conflict had become a destructive part of their church life.

I did little structured mediation as a serving archdeacon or bishop; there was rarely the opportunity to spend the unhurried time needed; and, in practice, the conflicting parties sometimes believed that the diocese was a party to their dispute, rather than an honest broker. I learnt to look beyond the presenting problems, to discern where the deeper concerns and challenges lay. This was particularly important in seeking to find appropriate support for the people concerned.

I recognized through my ongoing relationship with Bridge Builders how important *good process* is in moving forward in conflict resolution. And in my senior leadership roles, I saw that sometimes poor process is the soil in which the seeds of conflict germinate and flower. Ignorance of established processes and occasionally the deliberate avoidance of such procedures can get people into trouble, setting up conflicts in areas such as employment or safeguarding. Those of us in senior leadership roles can help to steer people in the right direction regarding tried and tested processes, without stifling the creativity that is so essentially the work of the Holy Spirit.

Over the years, it's become clearer to me that local church leadership requires a high degree of emotional intelligence and a good dose of courage. In engaging with those caught up in dispute, I found it important to work with their emotional responses to their situation. This was because their conflicts were, often unwittingly, fuelled by a sense of personal pain or grievance. Too few congregation members are aware of the costly emotional engagement faced by ministers and their families. I was therefore glad when, as a senior leader, there was the opportunity to provide help for ministerial colleagues. Such help is particularly needed when they've come under severe personal pressure arising from an outbreak of intense conflict in their church.

Can you think of examples where exploring people's feelings helped to release a way forward?
I sometimes found myself early onto the scene of a burgeoning church conflict. I remember a group of rural churches which

was thrown into confusion when their organist was accused of a safeguarding breach in another place where he taught music. Adamant that he was the answer to their prayers, people felt angry when he was suspended pending time-consuming police inquiries. In subsequent stormy meetings of lay leaders, early on I gave the opportunity for them to express their feelings. This began the process of understanding why they were so distressed; and helped me offer a considered response, as the full story unfolded. It was tempting to dismiss the intense feelings. Had I done so, this would have alienated many good people who sensed being out of their depth. Without that early surfacing of feelings, a tricky situation could have become a worse crisis; and the way forward would have been harder to discover.

How were silent presence and touch part of your ministry among those working through conflict?
Silence, and sticking with it, can allow the real questions people are asking to come to the surface. I found that being quietly attentive to others gave them the space to formulate words – or to allow emotions to rise to the surface. Pastoral ministry furnishes many opportunities to offer this quiet attentiveness. For example, deep stories can emerge when a bereaved family is given space to express themselves; or a painful admission can be tearfully shared when the minister graciously attends to the person, rather than watching the clock.

Conflicts are part of the lives of diverse relational groups – families and churches. Group members can feel a loyalty that prevents them from disclosing something which could be uncomfortable for another person. The silence and attentiveness of a less anxious presence can lower the defensive threshold. Such presence can help people to be more honest, as well as creating a calmer atmosphere for the needed conversation.

Silence is a special gift when there is a significant power differential between the parties: there were many occasions when I discovered the importance of waiting for a reticent participant to speak, especially when there was pressure from a more bullish person for us to 'get on with it'.

Touch can be as significant as silence. As a bishop some of the eagerly anticipated events in my diary were confirmations. People sometimes described the moment when hands were laid on their head, during the bishop's confirmation prayer, as a profound spiritual experience. On one occasion, I had the privilege of confirming a terminally ill 84-year-old man. Before the service, he told me that he'd felt guilty ever since bunking-off confirmation classes when he was a boy of 14. After seven decades, he'd finally plucked up the courage to admit his sense of guilt and to seek the blessing of the Holy Spirit. As I lifted my hands from his head, he kept saying 'I don't believe it,' while chuckling in an infectious way. He couldn't believe that he'd come back to God at last. As his inner conflict was resolved, what emerged was laughter: pent-up emotions released in the joy of meeting the Lord who loved him deeply. It was a heart-warming occasion for his family and neighbours, and a delight for me to witness. Hence the tactile dimension of confirmation has always been important. It resonates with New Testament evidence of the sharing of the Spirit.

I'd add that silence and touch best come from *within* those ministering: they can't be forced or imposed, as that would be coercive and would lead to the loss of their intrinsic value.

What has helped you to befriend silence? Why does it matter?
Watching the culture around me, I see so many people – and indeed some churches – filling every moment of their lives with noise. Over the years, it's convinced me that there must be something better than such 'addiction to distraction' if we are to make sense of our precious yet puzzling lives.

I'm married to someone for whom silence is a trusted friend; and over the years we've found the blessings of what we call 'companionable silence': the quiet enjoyment of each other's company while travelling or doing some shared task. I've gained so much from being close to someone who values silence.

I've also been privileged to have close connections with religious orders and, over time, the silence they practise has quietly stolen into the way I organize my own life. To someone who is an activist, never happier than with jobs to do, the gift of silence has deeply enriched me. I reflect on how few words Jesus spoke when ministering to others, and yet how effective his ministry was: I believe there is a connection between the two.

A Theological Reflection:

Matthew 17.1–8 (The transfiguration of Jesus)

Mountain-top spiritual experiences can be bewildering. This is the case for Peter as he and his two closest colleagues witness Jesus' transfiguration. They see Jesus' face glowing like the sun. Have you seen someone whose face is radiant? A child who knows their parent's pleasure; or an athlete who has won the trophy. We can imagine that Jesus' appearance was something like that, only amplified. The radiancy dial was turned up to maximum. And the mountain setting was a clue that this radiance displayed the glory of God.

The excitement does not end there. Suddenly Peter and his two friends see Moses and Elijah talking with Jesus: Moses, who represents the covenantal law of Israel, and Elijah, who embodies God's prophetic word spoken to the people. No wonder Peter thinks this is a moment worth prolonging, even if he is too quick to speak. But before he can finish, a bright shining cloud appears and overshadows them all. And then another voice speaks. It is the voice of God. A voice that identifies Jesus as God's Son, and that tells of God's delight in him. A voice that then gently but firmly commands the disciples to listen to Jesus. It is no surprise that Peter and the others are terrified, falling on their faces.

This is when Jesus acts. He does four things.[2] First, he moves to be alongside Peter, James and John. He does not speak from a distance. Rather he draws physically close, while remaining silent. Then, before he says anything, he touches them. A touch that reassures them that he is at hand. A touch that expresses his care for them. A touch that reminds them of his humanity. Then he speaks, inviting the disciples to stand up. In the midst of their fear, he helps them to their feet again. Finally, he speaks, saying, 'Don't be afraid.' The disciples can now hear this message. They can hear it because they have felt Jesus' quiet presence, they have known his gentle touch and they are now upright again. He has articulated their strongest feeling – and they need be afraid no longer.

When we face times of conflict, in which we are wrestling with our fears, it is God's close presence with us, and God's reassuring touch, that can calm us. For us to feel this, the presence and touch may well need to be expressed through a human agent, as was the case for Peter and his friends. That is what will allow us to stand upright and not be frightened. In journeying through our conflicts, it is this presence and touch that we can helpfully offer in ministry to one another. In doing so, we may catch a glimpse of God's glory.

Notes

1 David Runcorn, 2017, *Silence: The Gateway to God*, Cambridge: Grove Books.

2 I am indebted to Sam Wells for this insight, given in an unpublished address for an ordination retreat.

8

Recognize the Limits

Are conciliation and mediation invariably good things? Sometimes senior church leaders seem to think so: 'This conflict has escalated to a serious level; we must try a mediatory approach.' It might seem churlish for an advocate of bridge-building to discourage this. However, in this chapter I suggest that there are limits to the use of a conciliation or conflict resolution process. We explore three different elements. First, how intense the conflict has become. Second, how a key player's personality or health may constrain matters. Third, an insight into why some conflicts can be so frustratingly difficult to work with.

A complicated case

One day I received a call from a senior church leader with oversight responsibility for numerous churches. He wanted to know whether Bridge Builders would mediate in a local church that was troubling him and which had taken up much recent attention. The following story emerged.

The minister of the church and his wife were going through a bitter divorce, with threatening letters being exchanged between their respective lawyers. The wife claimed that her husband had emotionally abused her – although she was unwilling to make a formal complaint to the police. The husband asserted that his wife was overwhelmed by bitterness, having never supported his ordained ministry; and that, over the years, she had increasingly resented all he had given in service of the church.

People within the congregation had taken firm sides, fuelled by views either of the minister or of his wife, freely shared with their respective friends. Supporters of the minister were profoundly grateful for him: they felt he had given sacrificially of himself in ministry. Indeed, many believed that he was the most Christ-like man ever to have served their church. They viewed the minister's wife as a malign force out to destroy him and his service of God's kingdom. Truth be told, they saw the wife as on the side of the devil; the sooner she was gone from their community, the better.

In contrast, supporters of the wife were convinced she had been criminally wronged by her husband, and that he should therefore be removed from ordained church ministry. They were righteous campaigners on behalf of a victim of abuse. They viewed those in authority, and the minister's supporters, as having been hoodwinked by a plausible hypocrite. They were convinced that the minister was a betrayer of his pastoral office and promises. So they were disappointed that the wife was unwilling to go to the police; but they were determined to try and prevent the minister continuing in ministry at their church – or indeed elsewhere.

Speed Leas' model of escalation

The question was, could Bridge Builders mediate in this situation? And if not, how did one discern what sort of alternative response might be appropriate? A model developed by Speed Leas, a North American church consultant, proved helpful.[1] Built on the assumption that there are stages to any conflict, his model distinguishes between them, and proposes that any intervention strategy needs to be tailored accordingly. Leas is convinced that a 'gut level' response is inadequate, and that objective criteria are needed to assess the level of a conflict's intensity. (There are other, more complex models.[2] Leas' is easier to grasp, and has proved practically useful to church consultants.)

Leas proposed five levels of intensity, which can be pictured as steps on a staircase of escalation (see Figure 8.1).

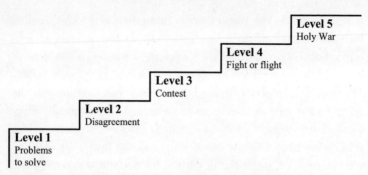

Figure 8.1: Based on Speed Leas' five levels of conflict.

Here is the dynamic at each level:

- *Level 1: Problems to Solve.* There are real differences between people, but those involved are problem-focused not person-focused. Communication is clear and specific, and people involved want to sort out the problem.
- *Level 2: Disagreement.* People are more concerned with self-protection than problem-solving and talk principally with their friends about how to address an issue. Communication is more generalized, and people withhold information that could be used against them by others.
- *Level 3: Contest.* People are focused on winning the argument and coming out on top. There is a win–lose dynamic. Communication becomes distorted, with personal attacks and emotional arguments overshadowing rational argument.
- *Level 4: Fight or Flight.* People's goal is to hurt or get rid of others; or to leave if they cannot achieve this. Factions have solidified, with identified leaders. The good of the subgroup becomes their focus, with no concern for the wider body. Communication is characterized by blaming, negative stereotyping, self-righteousness and a refusal to take responsibility.
- *Level 5: Holy War (Intractable).* People's goal is to destroy one another. They see themselves as part of an eternal cause, fighting for universal principles. They justify any means to achieve their all-important ends. Communication features outright condemnation of others, and extreme

emotional volatility. People are unable to disengage. (Leas designated this level as 'Intractable'; I prefer church consultant David Brubaker's re-designation of 'Holy War'.)

Levels 1 and 2 are normal levels of church conflict. Level 3 is common and is the first level where participants name the dynamic as one of 'conflict' or dispute, because negative elements become more evident. It is less common for churches to reach Level 4 – but once they do so, people generally feel stuck. Level 4 is when a church will normally need outside help to find a way forward together. Church splits can happen at this level, either at a local congregational level, or at a larger denominational level. Level 5 is conflict at its most destructive. At this level participants engage in vicious or even violent behaviours towards one another – even if everyone sees themselves as faithful Christians. Once reached, at this level participants can no longer access a reasoned approach and have lost capacity for critical self-reflection. Instead they see themselves as a part of a great cause, fighting for unambiguous principles.

Applying Leas' model

Arriving at an accurate assessment of the intensity level is critical to determining an appropriate way of working with a conflict. Pause for a moment: try to work out the conflict level of the case with which we began this chapter . . . It is not straightforward.

Misjudging the level risks proposing an approach that may, at best, be ineffective; and which could well make matters worse. Bridge Builders therefore developed a set of five criteria to help in making an assessment, grounded in these questions:

- What are the participants trying to achieve?
- What approach are they taking to the situation?
- How are the participants communicating with one another?
- What is the make-up in terms of the group and subgroups?
- What core convictions do participants hold about the situation?

Here is my analysis of our case study. In terms of the *parties' goals*, there are signs that the wife and her supporters are seeking to destroy the minister – at least, they are trying to prevent him continuing in ordained ministry. This suggests Level 5, 'holy war'. The goal of the husband and his supporters is to see the wife leave, pointing to Level 4, 'fight or flight'. However, their *language* has moved beyond negative stereotyping to outright condemnation, pointing to Level 5. There are clear *factions* which have formed on both sides; but these have not yet solidified into ideological organizations strategizing how to harm the other side. This points to Level 4. When it comes to the parties' *convictions and assumptions*, both sides see the other as hypocritical; but neither has reached the point where they cannot stop fighting and would rather die than give up. This, also, points to Level 4. Overall, my assessment was that, looking at the 'critical mass' of the people, this was a high Level 4, 'fight or flight' conflict.

(A complicating factor is the possibility that the minister may be guilty of emotionally abusing his wife. If true, this would call for a process of repentance and rehabilitation, rather than a standard conciliation process.)

After building up a picture through a long interview, my advice to the senior leader was that a reconciliation process with the local church would be unwise until the minister and his wife had both moved on. At that point it could be worth investing in a process to restore relationships between the remaining members of the congregation. A process of mediation could potentially be used between the husband and wife, led by trained family mediators; however, I suggested that, once things had escalated to an exchange of threatening solicitors' letters, with factionalized supporters on both sides, there was not much hope of success.

Broadly, Leas' model points to the following intervention options:

- *Levels 1 and 2: a dialogue*; no external intervention needed.
- *Level 3 'contest': a structured process of dialogue and problem-solving*, with some skilful facilitation, is needed.

Where the expertise is missing in the group, a suitably trained external person can helpfully lead the process. Alternatively, resourcing the participants to facilitate their own situation is more empowering.

- *Level 4 'fight or flight': external assistance is required*, as no one inside the situation is seen as impartial. However, a mediatory intervention may not be appropriate, as our case study illustrates. The longer things have run, and the higher the level of intensity, the less likelihood that a conciliation process might succeed.
- *Level 5 'holy war': separating warring parties and removing key protagonists from the front line* is needed. This calls for an exercise of authority, where available, and a setting of limits. A process of conciliation and facilitated dialogue will be fruitless: a waste of time, energy and money, because the parties have lost the capacity for rationality and self-reflection needed for a dialogical process.

Condition of a key player

Speed Leas' conflict levels help to explain why some group conflicts are so hard to work with: they are highly escalated. However, there are times when working with a conflict is inhibited mostly by one key protagonist. This partly depends on the structures, and on the balance of power within them. For example, within the Church of England, the incumbent of the parish has a role as vicar or rector from which they usually cannot be removed unless guilty of serious misconduct. They hold significant positional power within their role.

I recall one problematic Anglican parish case. While leading a parish reconciliation, the facilitators puzzled to make sense of the vicar's behaviour, both as reported to them by parishioners, and from their observation. Eventually they wondered whether the vicar was exhibiting signs of high-functioning autism. This made sense of his apparent insensitivity, and of some strange or socially inappropriate behaviour, especially when he felt blocked by others. (There were some family clues which reinforced this possibility.) In an individual coaching session, one of the facilitators tentatively broached this suggestion with the vicar, and asked whether he might consider seeking a medical diagnosis. The vicar quickly dismissed the idea and resisted any possibility of exploring it. The facilitator wondered whether the vicar might at least consider strategies available to assist those with high-functioning autism, which might help him in his interactions with parishioners, if he was willing to try them. The vicar was unwilling.

While Bridge Builders completed the parish reconciliation process and helped many parishioners achieve greater mutual respect and understanding, and find some healing, the process only had a limited impact. My assessment was that the main stumbling block was the vicar's condition, and his refusal to face it. Sadly, we heard that the parish's situation later went further downhill, apparently because the vicar was unchanged in problematic interactions with parishioners and remained blind to his contribution.

Although not a frequent occurrence, I have encountered other cases where a key player inhibited reconciliation. The common factor was the person being in an influential position from which they could not be readily moved; and that they had an apparent personality condition, such as autism, or a significant health issue, which they were unwilling to acknowledge. So, they would not seek help to address the condition, thus preventing the possibility of growth or change.

There is a flip side to this: a tendency for people to quickly *label* someone whose behaviour they find difficult. Perhaps, saying they are 'on the spectrum'. Or, another favoured one, 'a bully'. Such labelling is often a way of trying to shift all the blame onto the other individual. Typically, it represents a refusal to take responsibility for one's own contribution to difficult interactions. I am as wary of this as of being blind to the – relatively rare – occasions when an unrecognized condition is a root of the challenge.

Difficult between-frame conflicts

We have considered how too-escalated a level of conflict can make conciliation inappropriate; and how a key protagonist can block the effectiveness of a conciliation process. We conclude by noting the limitations of what one might call 'conventional conflict resolution' – the approach that assumes one can identify key issues and underlying concerns to be addressed and can then negotiate specific actions to resolve them, which all can affirm.

In practice it can sometimes be a challenge to get anywhere near doing this. The work of the sociologist Penny Becker is helpful in explaining why. Her insight emerged from research exploring the patterns of conflict among 23 congregations in an American city. Becker identifies a distinction between 'within-frame conflict' and 'between-frame conflict'.[3] A *within-frame conflict* results from a violation of shared expectations, whereas a *between-frame conflict* results from the clash of two fundamentally different sets of behavioural expectations. Within-frame conflicts can be resolved by standard processes of negotiation and compliance and are relatively straightforward to deal with. Between-frame conflicts are more difficult to resolve because the different sets of expectations mean there are divergent views on how to reach a decision. Becker concluded that between-frame conflicts are often fundamentally about identity and culture. Those involved in such conflicts are wrestling with fundamentally different answers to the questions 'Who are we?' and 'How do we do things around here?'

Becker's distinction is reflected in research on international conflict, in the difference between 'interest-based conflicts' and 'identity-based conflicts'.[4] *Interest-based conflicts* have defined and concrete issues. Desired outcomes are based on tangible interests and resources; and there is a common view on how to interpret the conflict and what could help settle it. In contrast, *identity-based conflicts* have issues that are abstract, complex, and difficult to define. It is hard to identify desired tangible outcomes. Such conflicts often involve divergent interpretations of history, culture, values and beliefs that seem to be incompatible – as we saw in Chapter 5 when considering the conflict in Northern Ireland. Identity-based conflicts hold elements that are essentially non-negotiable. Such conflicts are not amenable to interest-based, problem-solving approaches offered by conventional conflict resolution. Instead, something like John Paul Lederach's approach to peacebuilding is needed, with a focus on transforming rather than resolving the conflict. This takes a long-term and multi-layered project of building relationships and understanding, alongside working at the problematic issues.

Recently, many church denominations have wrestled with issues around human sexuality and identity; in particular, how to view same-sex intimate relationships. There are indications that this conflict bears the hallmark of an identity-based, or between-frame, conflict. Among disputing Christians on this issue, there are some striking differences. There are differing views on how to read and interpret the biblical Scriptures; and on whether sexual orientation and gender identity is innate or chosen. Some see the Church in danger of accommodating to society's prevailing culture; others see the world as having something prophetic to say to the Church. There are divergent views on what faithful discipleship looks like for Christians in relation to their sexual orientation and gender identity. There are differences about whether to place God's original creation at the centre of the story, or whether to place our heavenly future with God at the centre. Cumulatively, these differences make it painfully hard to reach an agreement on how to settle the issues in a way that both 'sides' can embrace. This is a classic between-frame conflict, which does not lend itself to conventional negotiation and problem-solving.

Only a challenging process of deep exploration and deeper listening offers the hope of transforming this conflict. Building bridges across such divides takes energy, stamina, commitment and courage; and a willingness to explore the complexity of our human identities and sexuality. It also takes wisdom in discerning how God is speaking to the Church today. Whether the will is there to keep building bridges remains to be seen. What is clear is that conventional conflict resolution approaches are inadequate. Only a dynamic peacebuilding approach will enable us to move forward together. In parts of the worldwide Church, people have already given up, and splits have then occurred. Looking at the Church of England, I fervently hope and pray that we can do better.

Recognizing conciliation's limits

We have seen in this chapter that there are limits to the use of mediatory process. Conflict can escalate to a stage of 'holy war' where dialogical processes are no longer effective. Reconciliation can be inhibited by a key protagonist who has a personality or health condition that they are unwilling to recognize. And some conflicts are of such complexity, that finding a way forward together will only be discovered through a costly and lengthy commitment to building relationships and understanding. There are times when conciliation simply is not enough, and we need to recognize its limits.

A conversation with Sandra Cobbin

Sandra is an independent trainer, coach and mediator, who runs her own company, Clarity Development. She works with church and charity leaders, and their teams, developing their skills and confidence. Sandra has been a training partner with Bridge Builders for several years.

How did you come into the field of working with conflict in churches?

A dozen years ago, I was working with a Church of England diocese that wanted to establish a diocesan mediation team. They asked if I'd be interested in being on the team. I thought, 'Why not?' All prospective mediators were then sent for training with Bridge Builders. This completely changed my life. It was an extraordinary experience, as if I began the training as one person and came out as another. I'd grown up in a family that avoided conflict; and I'd also been affected by my first marriage ending in

---

divorce. At the course beginning, my image of conflict was of two trains smashing together: absolute carnage and destruction. A week later, my image was of a road with possibilities and opportunities emerging from conflict. I'd never thought of conflict as something within which one could find a nugget of gold, of life or hope.

I wanted to take it further, because of things God had put his finger on and my new understanding. I attended further courses that kept the content alive; and, later, co-trained with Bridge Builders' staff. This has taken me on a journey of self-discovery, in which I've learnt new things about God. I've found that I can make choices in how I relate to others and in my attitudes. I continue to find insights from my training to be real, earthed and transformational. And Jesus' prayer in John 17 has become a compelling text for me: it's in the way we love one another that we reveal God's love to the wider world.

As a trainer and facilitator, I want to share this learning with Christians. I delight in seeing how the insights can transform other people's lives, as they have mine.

What's it like for people being part of an intense, escalated conflict? What does it take to survive this?
From working with churches in such situations, I've noticed that it's a costly place for people to find themselves in. There's an emotional cost to the brokenness of relationships. There's an intensity to people's feelings; thinking about the situation can become all-absorbing. Over time, it's an endurance test, with an emotional, physical and spiritual cost.

As Christians, we typically believe that we should be nice to one another. There's therefore a profound sense of disconnect when we're in an intense conflict with other believers; our experience somehow contradicts our faith. It challenges us, raising questions about our identity, because it feels that Christians shouldn't disagree so fundamentally. While Jesus calls us to love our enemies, the idea of finding another Christian as our apparent enemy can feel wrong.

The Psalms can be an extraordinary resource amidst intense conflict: they give voice to what we might want to happen, to our cry for justice. They give permission to call someone my 'enemy', part of expressing that cry. I recall someone in such a conflict realizing that the psalm they'd found helpful could be the very prayer that their 'enemy' was finding helpful as they thought about them! That was a turning point.

The Psalms give us a voice in conflict, because they're a heart cry between the individual and God. Walter Brueggemann helpfully suggests that, when we pray the tough stuff in the Psalms, we're trusting that God will act lovingly and in a just way. We can say that we want these people to suffer, while knowing that, being loving and just, God will not simply do what we say. Rather God will act out of deep love and justice, both for ourselves and for those with whom we're in dispute.

I've observed that, when we're part of an escalated conflict and seeing the other person as the enemy, we can lose sight of 'them' being a person like me, made in God's image, someone whom God loves. When entangled in intense conflict, we lose empathy and can hurt others without feeling bad about it. A key moment of transformation comes when we rediscover the other's humanity, amidst God's mercy. Without that, we'll struggle to stay open, relational and respectful. It's a spiritual discipline: reflecting on the breadth of God's love and concern for every person, including those opposing us.

There's a special cost for a minister, as the primary leader, when they're caught up in a 'fight or flight' conflict. There's a difficulty of disengaging, expressed as a worry about even taking a day off. In coaching them, I'll be asking: 'Where are your places of rest? Your rhythms of sabbath and retreating?' 'Where's a safe place to articulate your difficult feelings – without hooking someone onto your side?' 'Who loves you unconditionally, who's good to spend time with?' and 'Who can bring you appropriate challenge?' Answering these helps a minister navigate through an intense situation, and build resilience and sustenance. At root, they're about finding a way to let go and entrust oneself to God.

How feasible is it to find a way forward in such intense conflicts?
I seek to be a hope-bearer. As I step into the conflict, I imagine myself stepping into the fiery furnace with Shadrach, Meshach and Abednego, looking for the presence of God. From the people involved, I'm looking for a willingness to listen, and to risk speaking openly. These are vital, to make any progress. One obstacle people can struggle with is the idea that the other person might fully understand what they're saying – but still not agree. There's often a sense that, 'If they really understood what I think, then they'd agree with me – because of course I'm right!' Mediatory efforts can stall at this point.

Some years ago, I was on the team of facilitators for the Church of England's 'Shared Conversations' process, exploring differences over human sexuality. The most life-giving and grace-filled moments – when heaven seemed to come to earth – were when people of profoundly differing views risked trying to understand one another and were able to say, 'I still don't agree with you and haven't changed my mind. But I thank you because I've understood in a new and different way.' That was about the encounter, the looking one another in the eye, doing the hard work of listening deeply, and even seeing the image of God in the other person. Such work is central to engaging well with our churches' most difficult conflicts.

When we encounter one another in this way, when we meet each other in our vulnerable humanity, then we can meet God's image in one another. When that happens, I've observed the possibility of transformation, and that gives me hope.

A Theological Reflection:

Acts 15.36–41 (Paul's split with Barnabas)

How do you overcome a betrayal by a member of your community? Barnabas managed this when he extended a hand to Paul following his conversion. Paul had come up to Jerusalem wanting to join the other Christian disciples. But they were frightened of Paul and could not believe he had become a fellow follower of Jesus. The memories were still fresh: Paul had been instrumental in persecuting and even executing some of their friends. Only Barnabas was willing to trust Paul: advocating for him to the Apostles. Barnabas' intervention made the difference, and Paul was accepted among the believers. This was not an isolated moment of allegiance. It was to Paul that Barnabas later turned when needing help in teaching the new Gentile believers in Antioch. In this way began a working partnership that endured for several years.

In Acts 15, the shoe is firmly on the other foot. Barnabas proposes that they take John Mark with them on their next missionary journey. However, Paul feels betrayed and let down by John Mark: he had abandoned them early in their first missionary journey (see Acts 13). Barnabas is following his long-standing pattern of reaching out to those who have fallen, wanting to give them another chance. And an additional factor: John Mark is a cousin of Barnabas. There is a family bond also at play. For Paul, the task takes priority over the relationship. In fulfilling the mission, he only wants dependable colleagues. The situation is exacerbated by the strain they have all been under during the church-wide conflict about including Gentile believers in the church. Paul is unwilling to listen to Barnabas' entreaties. As a result, he and Barnabas split up and go in different directions. The book of Acts lacks any evidence that they ever resumed working – or even relating – together.

The reality is: Christians fall out with one another. There are times when a disagreement reaches such a pitch that the only realistic way forward is a parting of the ways, with as little bitterness and recrimination as possible.

However, does that need to be the end of the story? Although Barnabas and Paul do not appear to ever resume co-working, there are hints in Paul's letters that he is later reconciled to John Mark. Paul urges Timothy to seek out John Mark and to bring him because 'he is useful to my ministry' (2 Tim. 4.11). And Paul sends greetings to the Colossian churches from John Mark – who is presumably therefore with Paul – urging them to welcome him if he visits them. We do not know how this reconciliation happened. Or, how many years passed. Maybe the breakdown weighed heavy on Paul's conscience. Whatever the reason, eventually they found a way to rebuild their relationship. Paul and John Mark were able, in this life, to know a reconciliation that we are promised will be fully realized in our eternal future with God. However, if, like them, we have been through a highly escalated conflict, we may only get there slowly. And probably only after listening to the quiet promptings of the Holy Spirit.

Notes

1 Speed B. Leas, 1985, *Moving Your Church Through Conflict*, Bethesda, MD: Alban Institute.

2 For example, the German author Glasl proposes a nine-level model of escalation, see: Friedrich Glasl, 1999, *Confronting Conflict: A First-Aid Kit for Handling Conflict*, Stroud: Hawthorn Press, pp. 83–106.

3 Penny E. Becker, 1999, *Congregations in Conflict: Cultural Models of Local Religious Life*, Cambridge: Cambridge University Press, p. 4.

4 Jay Rothman and Marie L. Olson, 2001, 'From Interests to Identities: Towards a New Emphasis in Interactive Conflict Resolution', *Journal of Peace Research*, 38(3), pp. 289–305.

9

Love Your Enemy

I wonder how much challenge you like to receive. When coaching a leader, I ask, 'So, on a scale of one to ten, how challenging are you prepared for me to be?' Those committed to their personal growth are always up for being stretched. Jesus is never embarrassed about challenging us, his disciples: he is always committed to our growth into maturity. And Jesus challenges us with a call to love our enemies. Now you might reasonably ask, 'So what does that look like then, to love our enemies?' That is the question we explore in this chapter. It is hard to picture such love, without illustrations to put flesh on the idea. So, we will hear four stories: starting big, at a national level, and ending small, at a domestic level. Then drawing out key threads and insights from the four narratives.

Nelson Mandela and the Afrikaners

In my lifetime, Nelson Mandela is renowned as a peacemaker. He was a leading figure in the movement to overturn South Africa's policies of racial segregation, known as apartheid. Early in his political life, he participated in violent attacks on physical infrastructure. Then, in 1962, he was arrested and sentenced to life imprisonment for trying to overthrow the state. Mandela was shut up for 27 years in the bleak and notorious jail on Robben Island, at the bottom of Africa.

While in prison, Mandela pondered what it might mean to love his enemies. He learnt Afrikaans, the language of those who were imprisoning him. He also read about Afrikaner history. Finally, on his eventual release from prison, as he was being driven away by car, Mandela deliberately chose to let go of the hatred he felt for his Afrikaner tormentors and jailers – his enemies.

Once president, Mandela made a point of keeping on key Afrikaner staff, such as John Reinders, chief of presidential protocol, who had served the previous two Afrikaner presidents. Reinders naturally expected to be ousted from his post under the new black president. Instead, Mandela invited him to stay, treating Reinders with great respect throughout his presidential tenure. When he later told others about this, the recollection brought tears to Reinders' eyes.

Mandela also understood the importance of symbolic gestures. So, he invited one of his former jailers to his inauguration as president of South Africa. Later, he donned a Springbok rugby shirt to demonstrate his personal support for the white South African rugby team, when his country was hosting the Rugby World Cup.

Desmond Tutu, the Anglican Archbishop and anti-apartheid campaigner, identified 'magnanimity' as Mandela's greatest attribute: the capacity to be kind and generous to an enemy or opponent.[1] It was Mandela's magnanimity, among his other qualities, that facilitated a relatively peaceful transition to democratic elections and to the ensuing black majority government in South Africa. Against the odds, Mandela and his government achieved a significant level of societal reconciliation, preventing a wreaking of revenge by the black population against the white. Although he did not adequately address all the chronic social problems facing his country, what Mandela achieved was remarkable. Key to his achievement was how he treated his enemies and opponents.

Jo Berry and Patrick Magee

For those of us in a British context, even those who campaigned against apartheid, Mandela's story may seem remote. A story closer to home may bring the idea of loving one's enemies into greater focus. This one is particularly pertinent for those of us who remember the violence of the Northern Ireland conflict.

Jo Berry is the daughter of Anthony Berry, a British Member of Parliament who was killed in 1984 by a bomb planted in the Brighton hotel that was hosting the Conservative Party annual conference. The bomb was placed there by Patrick Magee, a member of the Irish Republican Army (IRA). Magee was targeting the then Prime Minister, Margaret Thatcher, who escaped the bombing physically unscathed. According to a message left afterwards, the IRA's attack was designed to send the message that Britain should not occupy the Republicans' country, torture their prisoners or shoot their people with impunity.

How did Jo Berry respond to the murder of her father by the IRA? She now found herself part of the conflict in Northern Ireland in an unexpected way. Suddenly it was personal. She says that within two days of her father's death, she started on a journey to try to understand those who had killed him.[2] She began visiting Northern Ireland to meet people caught up in the conflict; and, in her conversations, she found an echo of the pain that she herself was feeling.

It was a long journey for Jo Berry. Around 14 years after the Brighton bombing, following the 1998 Belfast Good Friday agreement, she suddenly saw Patrick Magee on television: he was being released as part of an amnesty for political prisoners. (He had earlier been sentenced to life imprisonment.) Magee was responsible for her father's death, and it did not seem right to her that he was being set free. However, over the next couple of years, the idea of *meeting* Patrick would not leave Jo's mind. She wanted 'to put a face to the enemy, and to see him as a real human being', as she later wrote.[3]

Two years after Patrick's release, their first meeting was arranged through a mutual contact, in the friend's home. Jo was frightened, and Patrick was overwhelmed. Jo was also curious, wanting to know who Patrick was beyond 'the Brighton bomber', a tag given to him by the news media. There was no one to facilitate the conversation, so they had to find their own way. They sat alone together for three hours, in a domestic conservatory, sharing their stories.

Jo talked about her relationship with her father and what he had meant to her. Patrick was surprised to hear what a fine person Jo's father had been – someone whose good qualities he could see in his daughter. Patrick then explained his reasons for joining the IRA, given what was going on in Northern Ireland. Due to her research, little was new to Jo. Then there was a turning point. Patrick fell silent. Disarmed by Jo's respectful listening, he said, 'I don't know who I am any more. How can I hear your anger and your pain?' He continued, 'I've never met anyone as open as you. What can I do to help you?' Jo describes it as a moment when the political mask fell off, and Patrick became a fellow, vulnerable human being. Their conversation changed: a truly human encounter had begun. Patrick moved from giving an account of his actions to offering an apology for having killed Jo's father. And eventually the conversation ended, with both exhausted.

They arranged a subsequent meeting. And, strangely, they kept on meeting. Their relationship developed until eventually they began telling their story publicly. For Jo, this was part of her peacemaking effort.[4] For Patrick, it was a contribution to reconciliation for the people of Northern Ireland. Together, they have now recounted their story many times, sitting side by side. In one seat, the woman whose father was killed by a bomb. In the other, the man responsible for that bomb. Sitting together and talking, quietly and respectfully. When I first heard them, I was deeply moved.[5]

For Jo Berry, the big question was whether she could let go of her desire to blame Patrick Magee for her father's death; and whether she could open her heart sufficiently to understand Patrick's motivation in resorting to violence. Through opening herself in this way, Jo discovered a compassion for Patrick. She came to recognize that had she and Patrick lived one another's lives, they could each have done what the other person did. Jo found a deep human empathy for the man responsible for her father's death. For his part, Patrick comments how rare it is to meet someone as gracious and open as Jo. He admits to being humbled by his encounter with her. His tone, and his presence when he sits next to her, match his words.

Jo Berry and Patrick Magee's story is remarkable: worth listening to and meditating on. However, it might feel rather outside our own experience. In our typical everyday interactions, in internal church situations, the hurts we cause one another might seem to pale into insignificance when compared to facing the person who has killed your parent, or whose parent you have killed. Yes, the hurts caused to those who have suffered sexual abuse at the hands of a church office-holder or a family member would fit into a similarly severe category. However, most other hurts are typically less serious, even if deeply felt.

Next are two stories of Christians who faced a hurt that affected them deeply. One was a marital betrayal; the other, a family conflict over a will. Neither is as dramatic as the preceding stories. But you may hear echoes of those stories, and recognize situations more typical of those you, and those you know, have faced.

Fiona and her husband, Giles

Fiona and Giles had been married for over 25 years when Giles came and made a confession: he told Fiona he had been having an affair with a work colleague. He had just ended the relationship but felt he must now admit what had happened. Fiona was distraught. She thought she knew her husband. He was a fellow Christian. They had worshipped God alongside one another their entire married life. Dozens of questions flooded through her mind. 'How could he do this to me?' 'Why didn't I realize what was going on?' 'What was wrong with me that he turned to someone else?' On and on went the questions. She found it hard to even look at her husband. They agreed it would be best if Giles moved out; so he went to stay with a friend who was willing to take him in.

When their only daughter heard the news, she was profoundly angry – more so than Fiona herself. She refused to even speak with her father. 'How could a man who says he's a Christian do this?' she said, 'He's just a deceitful fraud.' Fiona found herself having to contend with her daughter's pain as much as her own. At times it was unbearable.

After some weeks, Fiona's initial shock subsided. She stayed in contact with Giles, through their mutual friend. Then she reached a decision: she did not want to see Giles as her enemy, despite his hurtful betrayal. Instead, Fiona wanted to see if she and Giles could rebuild a relationship of trust. She was unsure how, but she said to herself, 'We've been married too long. We've been through too much to throw it all away.' However, she faced opposition from her daughter, who thought Fiona should end the marriage and start afresh. That made it harder for Fiona to seek a rapprochement.

Fiona was resolute; but realized that she and Giles needed help to have some difficult conversations. They agreed that working with a marital counsellor would assist the dialogue. At the start, Fiona needed answers to her questions. 'How often had Giles met privately with his colleague? Where had they gone together? How far did they go sexually, and how often?' Some of the answers were less bad than Fiona feared. But learning the detail also made her angry, and she felt more hurt – or was better able to express her pain, within the space created by the counsellor. Helpfully, Giles took responsibility for what he had done, and avoided excusing himself. He was honest about how the relationship had evolved and how he had got caught up in the subterfuge. He was also contrite, genuinely sorry for what he had done, and for the evident hurt he had caused Fiona. It was hard for him to see her suffering so.

In subsequent sessions, the counsellor helped them move on to other territory. What had they most valued about their marriage? What memories did they treasure? What struggles had they faced as parents? Gradually, as they explored their shared history together, Fiona began to look at Giles differently. At the beginning, she hated him. She hated what he had done to her, and to their daughter. Now, she began to see Giles as the fragile human being she knew him to be. Recognizing his fellow humanity, and remembering what she valued about their married life, eventually created a shift. Fiona started to believe they could have a future together again; she no longer saw Giles just as someone who had caused her unimaginable pain. She recognized her own weakness; and how, in Giles' position, she might have fallen prey to the same temptation.

They developed a plan for a gradual reconciliation. After the work with the counsellor, Giles would move back to the couple's home. But he would sleep in a separate bedroom. They would eat together, and start doing things together again. But they would not resume more intimate relations until Fiona felt fully ready. As time progressed, Fiona found herself looking more warmly at Giles, blaming him less: trust was returning. Although their daughter took much longer to soften towards Giles, within a year, Giles and Fiona were again living together as husband and wife.

Mark and his step-father, Charles

The last story is of a family conflict. Mark's grandfather, with whom he had enjoyed a close relationship, died. His grandfather had named his grandson as one of his executors, along with his eldest son, thinking it good to have executors from two different generations. What the old man had not thought through was the power differential. Mark was left dealing with people of an older generation: his two uncles, his mother and his step-father, Charles.

The big issue concerned the sale of the family home, which included a small orchard. Any developer would want to get planning permission to build some other houses on the plot. Early on, Charles – not an executor – took control of proceedings. He believed he could secure a good price for the property through his contacts. He persuaded the senior executor, but Mark was opposed: Mark thought the house should be sold on the open market, to get the best price. As an executor, he had a legal duty to maximize the return from the sale for the beneficiaries: his mother and two uncles. The younger uncle, the least well off, agreed. Two sides had formed.

But Charles moved quickly. Within a couple of weeks, he had received an offer from a national property developer of over £1,000,000. This was more than anyone expected. Charles was compelling, and stressed that the offer would not stand for long. The older brother and the sister, Mark's mother, wanted to accept the offer. However, Mark resisted the pressure, insisting they should put the house on the open market, to try and secure a higher price. There was an impasse.

Mark was angry that his step-father Charles had usurped his role as an executor. He also felt that Charles dishonoured Mark's grandfather, who liked things done 'by the book'. To Mark, Charles seemed like 'the enemy'. Mark's mother complained bitterly against him. The bad feeling escalated.

At this point, the younger of Mark's uncles took the initiative. He explained the situation to a small local property developer, who came to look at the site – and then offered £150,000 more than the other bid. Charles' contact would not match this. The younger uncle was happy with the increased offer – as were his sister and older brother. Mark concluded there was no need to press for an open sale. A private sale went ahead.

But Mark wondered what to do about his relationship with his step-father. There was still bad feeling on both sides. After a breathing period, Mark requested a meeting. He suggested seeing Charles alone, without Mark's mother present, but at their home. It was an awkward meeting. Mark listened to Charles, who felt vindicated, convinced that they had only got such a good price thanks to his action. Mark expressed his concern at how Charles had handled things: the confusion of roles, lack of consultation and the short-circuiting of good process. He also expressed regret, admitting he could have tried to maintain better relations. Charles accepted the apology; but offered none of his own. Mark left dissatisfied.

What was Mark to do about the hurt that he still felt, and his step-father's unwillingness to accept any responsibility? As a Christian, he decided that he wanted to let go of his bitterness; and to build a new relationship with Charles. It was not easy and took several years. Gradually, Mark developed a respect for his step-father. And, looking back, he could also see that, had he been in Charles' shoes, he might have acted the same. He was learning to love the one he had thought of as his family enemy.

The journey of loving an enemy

I wonder if you notice some threads running through these stories. Reflecting on them, let me offer eight observations about the journey of reconciliation.[6]

1 *Anyone who hurts us can become an enemy in our own minds* – from someone we have never met to a close relative. The scale of the hurt may determine the length of journey involved in overcoming our enmity. Individuals' capacity to make such a journey will vary. (Some may not start this side of the grave.) If we want to embark on overcoming the enmity, then we are wise to recognize that it may take a long time. For Mandela and Jo Berry, decades were needed. For more minor hurts, it can still take years, as Mark found in rebuilding a relationship with his step-father. Fiona was able to move more quickly, but she had a quarter century of positive memories acting as a counterbalance.

2 *There is often a period of withdrawal following a hurt or injury.* This may be a physical withdrawal, avoiding the one who has injured us. Or it may simply involve drawing back emotionally. Whichever, this is a normal human response, and not one to be frowned upon. Part of a self-protective instinct, it is best not avoided.

3 *When someone has been hurt, they need to articulate their painful feelings.* We may get to communicate this to the person who has hurt us – or we may not. But we will need to express those difficult feelings somehow. Maybe not in words, although finding some words is usually helpful. One person, uncomfortable talking about her feelings, expresses them through art work. This is her way of 'speaking out'. (How others are then able to 'hear' what she is expressing is a different challenge.)

4 *There is usually a decision point.* When we have been hurt, this is the moment when we resolve to find a way forward for ourselves – a way to overcome our enmity. Mandela took his decision as he was driven away from Robben Island. Jo Berry decided within a couple of days of her

father's death; and made a further decision after seeing Patrick Magee released from prison. Fiona and Mark both made their decisions after a few weeks.

Such decisions will be tested. Mandela and Jo Berry had to maintain their resolve in the face of ongoing opposition and criticism from their supporters. They both faced accusations of betrayal. Fiona's resolve was acutely tested by her daughter. This is the hidden cost of loving one's enemy: one's family, friends or allies may not like it. (There is a close connection between forgiveness, on which others have ably written, and loving one's enemies.)[7]

5 *The hurt party typically needs to take the risk of encountering the person perceived as their enemy.* The degree of risk will relate to the degree of hurt. If the offender has killed your father, the risk may be vast. If the offender has acted precipitately and without thought for you, the risk may be small. But there is always risk in undertaking a face-to-face encounter.

6 *It makes a big difference if the person causing the hurt expresses genuine regret, without trying to justify their actions.* Initially Patrick Magee sought to justify what he had done as the reasoned political act; but he was undone by Jo Berry's attention and deep listening. Giles was contrite from the outset, and took responsibility for his betrayal, and this eased Fiona's journey. However, there is no guarantee of contrition. As Mark found, the one who has caused hurt may not take any responsibility for the impact of their words or actions. Yet, as an injured party, Mark's own resolve to rebuild a respectful relationship was enough to see him through.

7 *A significant moment is reached when the hurt one recognizes the frailty and humanity of the one who has hurt them* – the one they saw as an enemy. This recognition of another's humanity involves finding sufficient empathy that we glimpse how, had we been in the other's position, we could – at least potentially – have acted as they did. Mandela worked at putting himself in his enemy's shoes by learning the Afrikaner language, by reading Afrikaner history, and by

building relationship with his Afrikaner jailers. Fiona, with her husband, and Mark, with his step-father, both reached the point of recognizing that they might have acted like the one who had hurt them. Jo Berry certainly reached this point, saying, 'There is no "other", no "enemy"; there is only the part of me that I know can be violent and that can act in a hurtful way.'

Berry's insight reminds us that the person we identify as an enemy may reflect an aspect of ourselves that we find uncomfortable to notice. Hence, learning to love one's enemy involves a journey of facing oneself in a new way, seeing oneself and the 'other' in a new light.

8 *It is possible to travel from a place of enmity to the point where a positive relationship is rebuilt with our opponent.* This will not be the same relationship as before. In Fiona's case, her relationship with her husband remained coloured by his betrayal; while, in other ways, they became closer than before. In Jo Berry's case, she built a relationship where none had existed before – to the point where she now calls Pat Magee her friend. These relationships were transfigured.

As well as loving our enemies, Jesus calls us to pray for them. While prayer was not an obvious feature of the four stories, it was certainly present. In Chapter 8, Sandra Cobbin observed how the Psalms can help us to pray when we face opposition from others. Fiona found this as she brought her situation to God in prayer. She discovered that, when she prayed for her enemy – her husband – honestly and openly, God began to transform her attitude to him. This is the Holy Spirit's work: changing, challenging and transforming us. Such transformation constitutes a mark of true prayer.

To many, the very idea of loving an enemy seems ludicrous. Yet, as we have heard, real, mostly ordinary people have resolved to move beyond hatred and to attempt the apparently impossible. The outcomes surprised them; and sometimes amazed those looking on. Learning to love one's enemy is a venture with many risks and no guarantees; but it gladdens God's heart and fulfils our Christian calling.

A conversation with Sarah Hills

Sarah is the Vicar of Holy Island, having recently served as Canon for Reconciliation Ministry at Coventry Cathedral. Prior to ordination she qualified in medicine and worked as a psychiatrist. She later completed a PhD on the theology of reconciliation and developed experience in working for reconciliation.

What drew you to want to work for reconciliation as the heart of your ministry, and how has this shaped you?

I first became interested in forgiveness and reconciliation through my upbringing. I was born in South Africa, and my parents were both involved in anti-apartheid activities. We left the country when I was young. In Northern Ireland, where we moved to, I grew up rather confused. About whether my hair was so curly because I was African; about why, when we went back to visit my grandparents, only white people could go to the beach or sit on public benches; about why my former nanny lived in a house with no running water.

After qualifying in medicine, I worked as a psychiatrist. My questions were given fuel when treating long-term illness through psychoanalytical psychotherapy. Several patients made significant progress towards healing once they forgave a perpetrator, a person who had hurt them, for example through maternal neglect or physical assault. I was left pondering: why was forgiveness crucial for some, but not, apparently, others?

As a curate on placement in Cape Town, I talked with many who'd been involved in the anti-apartheid struggle, who were still working for reconciliation in South Africa. Yes, apartheid had ended, and a new 'rainbow nation' had been born. However, there was still a huge racial divide marked by massive socio-economic and educational inequalities. The Truth and Reconciliation Commission made possible significant strides forward, helping to avert the 'bloodbath' that many feared. Yet, sadly, many of its recommendations were never implemented.

Later, I was delighted to take up the post of Canon for Reconciliation at Coventry Cathedral. The cathedral has been following a call to the ministry of reconciliation since its destruction during a bombing raid in the Second World War. Inspired by the example of the then head, Provost Howard, the cathedral helps people to work at forgiveness, and build bridges with former enemies.

What do you think it takes to love someone with whom one has been at enmity?

Paul Oestreicher, a predecessor of mine at Coventry Cathedral, defines reconciliation simply as 'the ability to love one's enemies'. This is much easier said than done. What reconciliation looks like is always determined by the particular setting and context. In my work, I've identified some key concepts – or provisional pointers – towards what's needed.

At its most basic, reconciliation is about sharing hospitality. It's about finding a way to welcome someone with whom we have a broken relationship – or with whom we didn't relate before. This is about discovering how to live better with 'the other'. The challenge is finding a way to construct the story of our lives so that we can relate to someone who's hurt us. Loving our enemies is not about ignoring the past. Rather, it's about re-membering the past, putting it together differently, developing a way to overcome the barriers in our hearts and minds, and imagining a new relationship with someone who's injured us.

A broken relationship has the possibility of healing and being mended. Like a broken pot that's glued back together, a fractured relationship won't be the same as before. But it can be something beautiful, if still fragile. This means finding a way to take steps that contribute to repair. These might include making the first move in meeting again: an offer of a cup of tea, or a safe enough space to get together to listen and talk things through – perhaps with another trusted person present. It's likely to involve acknowledging that hurts have happened and wrong been done. It might mean offering an apology. Hard as it may be, it may mean praying for 'the other': giving the situation to God and asking for a greater sense of the bigger picture, beyond our own perspective. Such are small – but significant – steps towards learning to 'love one's enemy'.

What can you offer for those wanting to be reconciled to an opponent, especially when their 'enemy' seems closed to this? It's worth appreciating that reconciliation is always a journey, and often a long one.[8] It may help to recognize that full reconciliation will not be achieved until the end of the story, the 'eschaton' when Jesus returns, and the earth and all humanity is renewed. However, that doesn't mean we can't move towards greater reconciliation in this life.

I distinguish between three broad types of reconciliation. First, is reconciliation between us and God. That's a doorway opened for us by Jesus. It can be a long journey before we find that doorway and can walk through it, but the doorway is always there. Second, there is reconciliation with one another – the focus of your question. There may be times when such reconciliation is not realistic, or even advisable, in this life. For example, where someone has been the victim of child sexual abuse, I'd not advocate reconciliation with the perpetrator – even though there can be rare, extraordinary occasions when this happens.

There's also a third type of reconciliation, within ourselves: a reconciliation with our circumstances. Situations will always arise where someone who's caused harm is unwilling to re-build a bridge, or who dies before that's possible. But some internal reconciliation is still possible. Even in situations as painful as recovering from sexual abuse, this can happen. It's never easy, and may take years. But it's possible. On this road, expressing anger may be important, as part of articulating one's pain; and lament, mourning all that was lost and that could've been. These stages of the journey may feel like low points, but it's important not to circumvent them. As we travel on, with the help of friends and those who care for us, we can find calmer places of green pasture and stiller water.

This road to internal reconciliation can bring a measure of healing that makes life more bearable; and a renewed joy-in-living

may spring up. One day – if only on the final day – I expect us to
reach the place where we find a table of welcome prepared for us;
and among those seated around the table will be those we once
thought of as enemies. To our surprise, we'll then find that our cup
then overflows with gladness. The hope of such reconciliation is
always worth the journey.

A Theological Reflection:

Matthew 5.38–48 (On avoiding retaliation or taking revenge)

It is hard to get more challenging than the teaching given by
Jesus to his disciples in his sermon on the mount. One of Jesus'
commands is particularly exacting: 'Do not resist an evildoer'
(Matt. 5.39). Or, perhaps more accurately, as one commenta-
tor translates it, 'Do not try to get even with the evil one.'[9] This
is a peacemaking command that teaches the Christian disciple
to avoid taking revenge or avoid retaliating against a person
who harms them. The harm may be against one's honour: the
slap on your face. It may be unfair treatment: taking your only
clothing. It may be someone exploiting their more powerful
position: forcing you to go a mile carrying their burden. It
could simply be someone taking advantage: begging for your
money or possessions.

When hurt or taken advantage of, the temptation – what
seems the natural and justified response – is to want to fight
back and retaliate ('an eye for an eye'). Alternatively, we can
be tempted to flee away and hide – and perhaps then plot our
revenge. Instead, whatever the harm done against us, Jesus calls
us to a step of non-violent resistance: turn the other cheek, give
the other garment, go a further mile, or offer another loan.
Each of these steps requires remaining present to the one who
has caused us harm and doing something surprising of our own
volition. Each such step confronts the other person causing the

harm with what they have done, but without resorting to harmful methods oneself.

Having addressed situations of everyday, occasional hurt, Jesus goes a stage further. Addressing the Christian community as a group, he says, 'Love your enemies and pray for those who persecute you' (Matt. 5.44). In the face of more sustained enmity, Jesus commands his disciples to 'love' their enemies. Part of this means praying for God's blessing on them, wishing them well and asking the One with power to use that power for our opponents' good. This goes against the grain and is challenging. It banishes hatred. It reverses an Old Testament trend of zeal against God's enemies. But it follows the logic of Jesus' earlier teaching about not seeking revenge against those who occasionally hurt us.

Jesus' teaching asks nothing of his followers that he will not have to practise himself. His teaching is prophetic of what he will endure in his final hours of earthly ministry: he is repeatedly struck on the face; he is stripped naked and humiliated; he is forced to carry a load that is not rightly his to bear; and he prays to God, asking God to forgive those abusing him. In his journey to the cross, Jesus shows us that God's way of love is to endure hurt and humiliation for our sakes. For we are all the ones who have been at enmity with God. It becomes apparent that magnanimity is one of God's central characteristics: loving enemies thus defines God, the God of Jesus Christ. Can we find ways to let it define us, as Christ's disciples? If we can, with the Spirit's help, then we will have matured into followers who more truly reflect the One we worship.

Notes

1 Quoted in John Carlin, 7 December 2013, 'Nelson Mandela: the freedom fighter who embraced his enemies' available at www.theguardian.com/world/2013/dec/07/nelson-mandela-freedom-fighter-john-carlin.

2 See the presentation at a conference marking the thirtieth anniversary of the Brighton bombing entitled 'Beyond Violence and Hate' available at www.youtube.com/watch?v=xknF_N9ihag.

3 See www.theforgivenessproject.com/jo-berry-patrick-magee.

4 See www.buildingbridgesforpeace.org/.

5 At the Greenbelt festival on 27 August 2018: their presentation was entitled 'Beyond Forgiveness: A Supreme Act of Imagination'.

6 I draw in part here on: Ron Kraybill, 'From Head to Heart: The Cycle of Reconciliation', in Carolyn Schrock-Shenk (ed.), 2000, *Mediation and Facilitation Training Manual: Foundations and Skills for Constructive Conflict Transformation*, Akron, PA: Mennonite Conciliation Service, pp. 31–3.

7 For a strong example, see: David W. Augsburger, 1996, *Helping People Forgive*, Louisville, KY: Westminster John Knox Press.

8 See: Brian Castle, 2014, *Reconciliation: The Journey of a Lifetime*, London: SPCK.

9 Frederick Dale Bruner, 2004, *Matthew: A Commentary, Volume 1: The Christbook, Matthew 1–12*, Grand Rapids, MI: Eerdmans, p. 246.

10

Build a Culture Together

An African proverb tells us that it takes a village to raise a child, the point being that we grow into maturity within the context of a wider community, not just a family. In this chapter I want to explore the shaping effect of church communities, and how Christians can develop a culture of peace in their life together. By 'culture' I mean the ways that we do things within a group: the patterns of behaviour, values and communication approaches that characterize us. I will draw on experience of the Mennonite tradition, which has shaped me.

Mennonite witness

In the past, when working at the London Mennonite Centre, I was sometimes asked how I got involved. My simple answer was that I married into the Mennonite Church. Sue, whom I wed in 1990, was part of the Wood Green Mennonite Church in north London. After our wedding, we committed ourselves to that small church together. I was impressed by their quality of relationships and commitment to Christian discipleship. As an Anglican, I knew little about Mennonites. Early in my involvement, it therefore helped to participate in a short course on Mennonites. As we explored some neglected sixteenth-century European history, I was struck by the witness of the early Anabaptist martyrs: their faith, love and boldness in the face of death shared qualities with the persecuted Christians of the early church. Yet, those insultingly labelled 'Anabaptist' were killed by both the Catholic and Protestant 'Christian' authorities of their day.

One story has stayed with me, about a Dutchman called Dirk Willems. It stuck because of an engraving that accompanied the story, easily found with an online search. The picture was of a man, on the edge of cracking ice, reaching out to help another who had fallen into the freezing water and who was about to drown. Dirk Willems was the man turning back to help. He was a Christian disciple – designated an Anabaptist – who had escaped from prison and who was on the verge of running away. His jailer, better fed and heavier, had pursued him onto the ice – which then gave way. The drowning jailer cried out for help. Willems responded to the cry and turned back. In doing so, he saved his jailer's life. Once safely ashore, the jailer was ordered to re-arrest the man who had saved him. Willems was then returned to prison; and later executed as a heretic.

The big question raised by the course leader was why Dirk Willems had turned back to help his pursuer. The jailer was likely to drown fast in the icy water. There was no time for weighing up options: Willems responded from a surprising reflex. The question was how he could have developed the habits that enabled him to respond to an enemy's cry for help. Two pointers were offered. One was the reality of the Dutchman's experience of Jesus Christ, whom he followed. The other was the shaping effect of the community of which he was part. 'It is probable that Dirk Willems responded as he did because he came from a particular kind of church, in which loving the enemy was an expression of loving the Lord, who had loved him to the end, and who had taught Dirk to love his enemies.'[1]

Dirk Willems' story is one that continues to shape the Mennonite Church, a Christian denomination that emerged from the disparate sixteenth-century Anabaptist movement. Spending time in the Mennonite congregation in London, I found myself being shaped by such stories. The son of a soldier, I had to rethink how I thought about the use of violent force and participation in the military. I concluded that the Mennonites were right in believing that faithful Christian disciples are called to love their enemies – and that this means forsaking any action to kill them. I embraced the identity of 'pacifist', believing that using violence and warfare to achieve our ends can never be justified. I was far from a natural pacifist: I knew my own forceful instincts, and my tendency to confront. But time among Mennonite believers nurtured a new commitment in me to abandon force and violence in more faithfully following Christ.

On 15 February 2003, I therefore marched with my Mennonite friends in public protest against the Iraq war. While many individual Christians took part in that great London march, our Wood Green Mennonite Church banner was one of few visible church banners on parade. It was there because the whole congregation had decided to join the protest, as part of the community's commitment to peacemaking.

Sometimes the small things are telling of a church's culture. In the Mennonite Church in London, I was surprised by the arrangement for making an announcement during the coffee time on Sunday morning. The church used what they called 'a silent shout'. When one person raised their hand high above their head, and kept it raised, others were expected to do the same – and to stop speaking as they did so. Everyone understood the system, so it was effective at achieving quiet, with visitors quickly catching on. It was respectful and empowering. It avoided people shouting to get a hearing. A child could initiate making an announcement, as sometimes happened. It was part of nurturing a culture of peace within the church.

One irony of the Mennonite tradition is that while its churches have been committed to a non-violent stance, they have struggled to deal well with internal tensions and disagreements. Down the centuries, this led to serious divisions, resulting in splits within the denomination. This is an object lesson: if the Church worldwide is to witness to the peace that Jesus brings, then Christians must find better ways to face internal church tensions and conflicts; and work them through in healthy ways. A new culture is needed.

A culture that nurtures peace

What might develop such a culture? Mennonite writers Alan and Eleanor Kreider, who worked in the UK for 30 years, have noted key qualities that are needed: a willingness to be vulnerable with one another; a humility to learn from one another and from how others may see things differently; a commitment to treating one another with respect, avoiding negative labelling; and a faith that holds onto hope in God's work of peacemaking in the world.[2]

As well as these qualities, to become effective peacemakers we need to learn from living examples (explored in Chapter 11), and from peacemaking communities. Part of the learning will be about improving our communication: developing deeper listening skills; and finding ways to speak up that avoid blaming and attacking others, while being honest about our own perspective and feelings. Further, there are other practical things a whole church can do to promote a culture of peace. Let us consider half a dozen of these.

Probably the most important thing is for ordained and lay leaders to *model healthy ways of engaging with disagreement and conflict*. What might this look like? A key element is moving towards those who disagree with you, rather than avoiding them. Which means listening deeply to others when they have a concern. This includes a willingness to listen to criticism of you as a leader, without getting defensive. It also means talking directly *with* others when you have a concern with them, rather than just talking *about* them behind their back. And it encompasses firmly but gently confronting someone's destructive behaviour where this is affecting others in a church.

None of this is easy, so it is wise to *provide skills training opportunities*. Such training need not be restricted to leaders but can be made available across a church. Ground that can usefully be covered includes:

- exploring people's attitudes to conflict and the way this is shaped by our family backgrounds;
- helping us to think theologically about conflict;
- improving our communication skills;
- finding ways to get unstuck when we have taken up antagonistic positions;

- learning to adapt our approach to conflicts according to the circumstances;
- recognizing how emotional process can trump rationality, along with exploring how to grow in emotional maturity; and
- identifying unhelpful patterns of behaviour within our group – and agreeing healthier ones.[3]

Critically, this means *agreeing how we will treat one another when we disagree*. Some years ago, the Mennonite Church in North America produced a statement entitled 'Agreeing and Disagreeing in Love'. This offers commitments for Christians to make to one another; and it is now available online as a model.[4] It includes guidelines on how to adopt the commitments in a local church. For congregations in the British Isles, the model will need adapting; but it can inspire us to develop our own version. And the *process* of agreeing and owning any guidelines will be as significant as what is agreed.

A piece of more general process is to *find ways to hold better meetings*. You will know how poorly some church business meetings can be facilitated and led. Why not learn skills and wisdom from others in the wider world?[5] For example, vary how conversations are held: not just plenary discussion but also interaction in pairs and small groups. This avoids only ever hearing the same few voices. Attention to good process ensures that working time together is spent more productively – and enjoyably! It also reduces the risk of tensions within the group escalating, and becoming difficult to handle, at a later stage.

Another aspect of good process is to *make major decisions consultatively and collaboratively*. Big decisions that will affect a whole church community are best taken slowly, with careful planning. Legally, the decision may rest with a governing body – a church council, for example. But you can still seek views and feedback from other church members. This will surface concerns and raise issues that might not otherwise have been addressed. There is a range of possibilities for securing feedback. A carefully constructed questionnaire is quick. But a series of small group meetings, which people sign up for, is likely to give better-quality feedback. Or – perhaps more efficient – hold a large group meeting and divide people into small groups for conversation around a table, each with a facilitator. Although this needs careful planning and can be hard work, it repays the effort involved, by preventing destructive friction later.

All of this can be undergirded by learning to *read the Bible through 'conflict lenses'*. The biblical texts are a rich resource for thinking about the complexities of human relationships and the tensions that arise among us. For example, the Council of Jerusalem, in Acts 15, when wisely read, is an instructive example of addressing age-old pitfalls.[6] The theological reflections in the present book seek to offer a model for this way of reading Scripture. They are based on questions that could be pursued in the contexts where your church engages with the Bible:

- How does this passage speak about human diversity and God's purposes in creating such diversity?
- In what ways is the text challenging us to think differently about engagement with tension over our differences?
- How do creativity and insight emerge from the conflicts depicted in our biblical stories?

The above ideas are not exhaustive; but they would make for a good start in building a culture of peace. You might also ask yourself:

- What songs do we sing that express the culture of peace we want to develop?
- What are we teaching our children and young people about how to address conflict and make peace?
- What stories do we tell about our church's history, and how we've navigated through past difficulties?

These point to other aspects of church life that contribute to forming its culture and to the stories we tell about ourselves.

An illustration: Jonathan's story

Here is an example of what trying to create a culture of peace looks like. Jonathan, a friend of mine, went to serve in a Church of England parish where some reconciliation work was needed. He understood that this was part of his brief. In conversation, Jonathan explained, 'I first attended a Bridge Builders course in 2002 and then got involved in the network. Several years later, I responded to a call to become vicar of a parish that had experienced some conflict.

'The presenting tensions had been between the previous vicar and lay members with leadership responsibilities. After my arrival, it became clear that people also fell into two groups in relation to what had happened: some simply wanted to move on, without engaging with it; while others needed to process their difficult past experiences. The breakdown in relationship between the last vicar and lay leaders had been compounded by how long it took senior leaders to get involved. By then, the vicar had decided to leave, and so did not participate in a listening process begun by the diocese. There was confusion, anger, secrecy and hurt within the church.'

How had Jonathan approached things when he first arrived? 'I saw that my first task was to listen and seek to understand the people. I visited everyone on the parish's electoral roll, to get to know them. I heard various stories. Some celebrated past achievements; others mourned difficult events and broken relationships.' How had he continued? 'I sought to be a calm, non-anxious presence within the church, and to model constructive behaviour. I aimed to be vulnerable, by being willing to respond to a critical person. Rather than being defensive or self-justifying, I'd invite the person to expand on their concerns. "Tell me more," was one of my key phrases.'

How else had he promoted a culture of peace? 'I encouraged people not to see differences as negative; but rather as having the potential for creativity and for fostering deeper respect for others. So, in individual conversations, in groups and in the congregation, I modelled a way of listening that allowed people to tell their stories. I also set up a broad worship planning group which reflected different preferences and styles. Together, we introduced a time during worship when people could share stories about their lives. This focused on how they'd seen God at work or were struggling to discern God's presence. I also met regularly with our staff team, which helped ensure good communication among key leaders.'

Had he received any support? 'Yes, I was fortunate in having a work consultant with whom I met every three months. It was invaluable to take a step back, and to ask myself what I was doing to promote peace. Those hour-long conversations helped me to ask insightful questions, illuminating what was going on in the church. They also clarified what I, as a leader, needed to do in working with the congregation.' What resources had he found helpful? 'We used the healthy churches materials, produced by Robert Warren and others, at a parish day early on in my time.[7] We also supplemented our healing training, from a charismatic background, to include a wider approach developed by Russ Parker.[8] Later, our new curate led a course looking at how we could be a welcoming church. That brought together diverse voices and experiences to test how welcoming we really were.'

Had Jonathan tried to bring together those with different views on the past? 'There was some correlation between the two groups I spoke of earlier and those who attended the two different services. These dated back to the 1990s and had been introduced by the previous vicar-but-one. The early service was traditional Anglican; the later one less structured and more influenced by charismatic renewal. Two years into my time, we began regular joint services: on Easter Day, Christmas Day, at Harvest Festival and other occasions. The aim was to build stronger relationships. Then, over time, the coffee break in between the two services became another way for people to get to know one another, breaking down barriers.'

Jonathan continued, 'After two years in post, I approached an outside facilitator about working with us to process hurts from the past. We then spent nearly a year in church council thinking, praying and talking through the idea. Although the need was obvious to me, I didn't want to pressure people, believing they needed to be ready to explore past pain. Eventually, there was a consensus to do so. We then embarked on a process of listening to past hurts, led by outside facilitators. This gave many people an opportunity to open up; and, for most, this was hugely positive. It proved a watershed in the life of the congregation. Like the journey through a bereavement, the process helped people to move from anger and grief through to acceptance. Once the process was completed, we found that we were all looking forwards, rather than back.'

What impact had his presence and initiatives made? 'The reconciliation process was important. However, promoting a culture of peace is a bigger, longer-term project. Some changes happened early on, as I was accepted as a calm presence who wasn't going to judge, take sides, or bring in major changes. I wanted to be a collaborative leader focused on building relationships and ensuring good process – rather than working for outcomes I'd already decided on. Other changes took longer, such as the healing process, which started three years into my time. For a few, this process was unhelpful: they just didn't want to revisit the past. Some had high hopes which the process didn't fulfil. But, for the vast majority, the process was cathartic and energizing. In addition, we held a weekend that included a day of teaching and healing, with the bishop present. Our bishop graciously acknowledged some failings of senior leadership in addressing earlier difficulties, and people appreciated hearing this.'

Beyond bringing healing, had he tried to develop people's resilience? 'I started on this towards the end of my time in the parish. Just before I left, we held a day for leaders using some of Bridge Builders' materials focused on accepting and working with difference, as well as understanding our own preferred style when there are tensions.[9] I'd originally planned to do this earlier on, and to follow up with further work for the whole church. I saw a need to build capacity for dealing with future conflicts. There was unfinished work there, by the time I left. But, overall, the church was in a much better place to welcome their next vicar than when I'd arrived.'

Jonathan's story illustrates that changing the culture within a congregation cannot be rushed; it is a long-term process that takes several years. His story also highlights the importance of timing, especially when it comes to facing hurt within a group and directly addressing painful past experience. Jonathan sought to create a culture of peace. Whether it becomes embedded will depend on how the lay leaders and the next vicar take things forward.

Sowing seeds

An individual can make a significant contribution to developing a culture of peace, especially when, like Jonathan, they have a leadership role or long-standing influence within a group. Leadership was important within the Mennonite community in London, as offered by Alan and Eleanor Kreider (see more below) and their successors. However, the culture of peace those Mennonite leaders sought to develop was only sustained once it became part of the life-blood of the young Mennonite congregation. That happened as everyone in the church saw it as part of their discipleship. For building peace and transforming conflict are never solo activities: they emerge out of work together. Then, as a group's culture develops, it shapes our individual habits and reflexes. That's what the story of Dirk Willems illustrates.

The isolated Mennonite congregation in London later declined and eventually closed. However, through the ministry of the Mennonite Centre, they sowed some significant peacemaking seeds that continue to bear fruit in churches across many traditions in the British Isles today. In various respects the Mennonite witness is a seed that has fallen into British and Irish soil and died; yet it continues to bear a harvest. Bridge Builders is one fruit, a ministry that in its turn continues to sow seeds to build a culture of peace. How is your church doing at developing this kind of culture?

A conversation with Ernie Whalley

Ernie is a retired Baptist minister. He served as Team Leader and Regional Minister of the Yorkshire Baptist Association from 1998 to 2012, and was President of the Baptist Union. Being brought up in Northern Ireland gave him a grounding in the desire to work for peace and reconciliation.

How did you first come across Mennonites and what did you learn from them?

During preparation for Baptist ministry, I heard about the influence of the Mennonites on early Baptists. However, I didn't meet a Mennonite Christian until the 1990s, when Alan and Eleanor Kreider came to work at the Northern Baptist College in Manchester. That's when the Mennonite seeds began to germinate in my life. With Alan and Eleanor as colleagues, my understanding grew. I sat in on courses which they led in their unique joint-teaching style.

I recall Alan and Eleanor's input on the 'culture of peace' and how they saw this as 'God's vision for the Church'. Windows opened on what *shalom* (peace) truly meant in the biblical tradition; and how true peace is central within worship, in living and in our working lives. Here was a 'jewel with many facets', encompassing well-being, holiness, wholeness, justice and relationships both within and outside the Church. The idea of 'growing peace' in churches drew me like a magnet.

Through my studies, the 'grace and peace' mentioned throughout the New Testament became a deeper reality. Just as striking was how this grace and peace were demonstrated in Alan and Eleanor's lives, shared in the church that I was pastoring. They modelled peace in their listening, and in attentive relationships with diverse people: some well-educated, others not. Such peace, woven into life, was transformative and infectious. It gave a fresh direction to my ministry as a pastor.

How did you get involved with working with conflict in churches?

'Are you a Protestant or a Catholic?' I recall being asked that question on the school bus in rural Northern Ireland when I was seven. I didn't know what it meant and didn't know how to answer. That night I asked my parents about it. They looked at each other apprehensively and tried to explain about tensions between Protestants and Catholics. Their account was shaped by the fact that we lived in a Catholic area but came from a Protestant tradition; and that we enjoyed good relations with the other local farmers, many of whom were Catholic families.

I was therefore brought up to respect and to learn to live with difference – and, ultimately, to celebrate our differences. This offered fertile ground, in my heart and thinking, for embracing peace and reconciliation when I came to live in England. But it wasn't straightforward. While preparing for Baptist ministry, I recall the eye-opening experience of a 'listening walk' with a charismatic Roman Catholic priest-in-training. We had experience of the charismatic movement in common. However, I still had blinkers from my past – which the Holy Spirit had to remove before I recognized him as a brother-in-Christ.

It was later, in 1997, that I attended a mediation skills course at the London Mennonite Centre, led by another Mennonite, Richard Blackburn. I discovered new tools for understanding the causes of conflict; and developed better skills for how to handle it. Soon afterwards, I was appointed as a Baptist regional minister covering north eastern England. I had oversight missionally and pastorally of 170 churches and their pastors. I soon learnt that, among the wonderful signs of the life of God's kingdom, there were also fractures in people's relationships, impeding the kingdom's growth. The Mennonite training then came into its own, in finding ways to bridge the breakdowns.

Nationally, Vivienne O'Brien and I were asked to lead a seminar on 'hurting churches' at the Baptist Assembly. We planned for up to 50 participants. So, we were staggered when around 500 turned up, about a quarter of the whole assembly. A vivid reminder of the need for better skills training in order to build a culture of peace within our churches, and why I see it as important. And it's not just Baptists: I know from conversations with senior colleagues in other denominations that their churches face similar challenges.

What have you found to be significant in developing a culture of peace within a local church?

I believe that the tone of life in the local church is set by the leadership, both ordained and lay. Leaders are in key positions to promote a culture of peace. Hence, I believe peacemaking skills need to be introduced when people are preparing for leadership. I'm therefore encouraged to hear how this is happening in some theological colleges. It's of paramount importance that peacemaking courses are not squeezed out of preparation for Christian ministry, but rather are promoted. How many thriving ministries have hit the buffers because of conflict in church life? Too many. How often have the brightest of visions been snuffed out by an inability to form strong relationships, and by a lack of peace-full insights? Again, more than I care to count.

So, during my time as a regional minister, we secured grants to help leaders attend Bridge Builders' courses. When taken up, this training proved of great benefit to both ministers and congregations. In addition, we ran one-day 'tasters' within the Baptist regions, open to all – to give lay leaders greater access.

Once these peacemaking skills are introduced, they need to be honed through practice and further development. It's helpful for people to undergo further training to reflect on their practice and to keep on learning. I'm therefore encouraged by the new network of peace and reconciliation centres developing across the UK, including the Blackley Centre in Yorkshire, where I'm involved.

Looking ahead, I believe developing peacemaking skills is a core element in building healthy kingdom communities that are committed to Christ, to sharing genuine good news, and to modelling a gospel of 'grace and peace'.

A Theological Reflection:

Acts 2.42–47 (Practices that shape communities of peace)

In Acts, the author Luke often refers to 'all', 'everyone' and 'the whole group'. The sense of corporate engagement is striking. In Acts 2, four communal practices are mentioned: listening to the Apostles' teaching; spending time together in fellowship; breaking bread together; and praying to God together. These practices bore fruit in a culture where people noticed the needy in their midst. Having noticed, the believers then acted to provide for the needy by selling their possessions. A strong culture developed of generosity and sharing one's resources (Acts 4.32–35). This culture was so significant that when one couple deceived the community about the resources that they were making available, it proved fatal (Acts 5.1–11). Their story illustrates that truth-telling was another component of the culture being nurtured. In both Acts 2 and Acts 4, Luke makes a direct link between the church's culture and its growth. This culture enables them to navigate constructively through the church-wide conflicts recorded in Acts 6 and Acts 15.

In our generation, making peace with one another can be a neglected aspect of 'the apostles' teaching' that we pass on. It was a priority for Jesus, expressed in the sermon on the mount and through challenges to the Disciples in how they treated one another; and modelled in how Jesus ministered. It was a priority for Paul, as he struggled to share the culture of the early Jerusalem church among the new church plants that he established around the Roman world. For example, Paul rebuked the Corinthian believers for the way that they celebrated their eucharistic meals without due regard to one another (1 Cor. 11).

We have parallels with the early church's communal practices: hearing a talk or sermon, sharing in a eucharistic meal together, seeking God in prayer, and spending time together – often with refreshments. The bedrock is there. Our eucharistic or communion meals can potentially also shape a culture of peace. We are typically invited to share the peace, which urges us to seek reconciliation when we have offended one another. In our liturgical prayers, we are reminded that Christ has sacrificed himself – while we were God's enemies – to bring an end to violence and our scapegoating of one another. We are all equally welcomed at God's table to receive God's forgiveness and to share in God's life. These can be vital reminders that our God is a peacemaking God, who invites us to make peace with one another. If we embrace this understanding, and live it out in our church communities, then we too may see a new generosity and sharing of our resources with one another. And if that happens, there's every hope that the Church will grow, and the word of God spread, in our age as in Luke's time.

Notes

1 Alan Kreider, Eleanor Kreider and Paulus Widjaja, 2005, *A Culture of Peace: God's Vision for the Church*, Intercourse, PA: Good Books, p. 54.

2 Kreider, *A Culture of Peace*, pp. 76–80.

3 This is all ground covered by the training resource: Alastair McKay, 2016, *Growing Bridgebuilders: Changing How We Handle Conflict*, Coventry: CPAS and Bridge Builders Ministries.

4 Available at http://mennoniteusa.org/wp-content/uploads/2015/04/Agreeing-and-Disagreeing-in-Love_11-2013.pdf .

5 For example: Michael Doyle and David Strauss, 1976, *How to Make Meetings Work*, New York, NY: Jove Books; Patrick M. Lencioni, 2004, *Death by Meeting: A Leadership Fable*, San Francisco, CA: Jossey Bass.

6 For one excellent exploration, see: John Paul Lederach, 2014, *Reconcile: Conflict Transformation for Ordinary Christians*, Harrisonburg, VA: Herald Press, pp. 109–23.

7 Robert Warren, 2012, *The Healthy Churches' Handbook: A Process for Revitalizing Your Church*, London: Church House Publishing.

8 Russ Parker, 2012, *Healing Wounded History: Reconciling Peoples and Healing Places*, London: SPCK.

9 McKay, *Growing Bridgebuilders*.

11

Observe the Peacemakers

'Blessed are the peacemakers,' says Jesus. But what *is* a peace-maker? How do we conceive of the work of peacemaking? In French, Jesus' blessing is rendered as 'bienheureux les artisans de paix': blessed are the artisans of peace. An artisan learns and practises a craft, beginning as an apprentice. This suggests that making peace requires training and practice. It takes time. And it requires learning from those who have mastered the craft.

In this chapter I want to share some wisdom learnt from others, especially from three experienced peacemakers: two North American Mennonites, John Paul Lederach and Carolyn Schrock-Shenk, and a Presbyterian from Northern Ireland, Joe Campbell, my formal dialogue partner at the end. I will draw on recent conversations with these crafts-people, in which I explored who they learnt their 'trade' from, and their observations on what makes for being a skilled crafter of peace.

Insights from John Paul Lederach

John Paul Lederach has worked internationally for 40 years in challenging situations of intense social conflict and civil war. In our conversation, he picked up on the idea of learning a trade. 'I like the notion of "craft". While we work to help people improve their skills, that can get reduced to the level of tech-nique.' John Paul continued, 'Craft captures the combination of skill and imagination needed to explore the deeper resonance that people have with each other – what I've called the art and soul of peacebuilding.[1] You have to bring into existence something that does not yet exist. It's more like an artistic process, creating a moment of insight, of "Ah, ha – *now* I have a better sense of it." It's also about creating hope, the hope that we don't have to be wrapped up in continuously repeating patterns that cause harm. The notion of a craft suggests opening a space that becomes generative, capable of new birth. That's critical in my mind.'

I wondered which peacemakers had particularly influenced him. He first mentioned Adam Curle, a British educator who worked in international peacebuilding over several decades, and a Quaker. 'It was not just his insightful writing,' said John Paul, 'but more the opportunities I had to spend time with Adam when I was younger, and he was in his seventies. He was an "elder wisdom-carrier" for me, imparting things that were significant for the whole of my life's work.' What things, I asked. 'A vision for the long-term nature of peacebuilding work, and a commitment to working in teams. Adam's understanding of conciliation was that it's about preparing people to enter into interaction more constructively with their enemies, with people they fear. He saw this sort of cultivation potentially taking years and years – and needing to be quiet work. It's about creating the safety for people to be more deeply reflective.'

Invited to say more about team-working, he said, 'The Quakers emphasized that peacemaking work requires a set of relationships where you're not isolated and alone, which is a recipe for disaster amid intense conflict. Adam observed that one's ability to hear and to see things improves exponentially when there are multiple eyes and ears. Too often people talk about the mediator in the singular. When working as a team, you're constantly in a process of checking out different ways of understanding, which has a greater depth to it. This contrasts with a single individual making heroic efforts in ploughing ahead, but who's really in an enormously fragile position.' He continued, 'We deeply underestimate the fragility that we experience when we have a proximity to human suffering.'

A second influence, said John Paul, was Elise Boulding, a pioneer in peace studies and another Quaker. 'Her notion of *prophetic listening* is that you listen in a way that whoever is talking has the opportunity to hear themselves – to hear, as she put it, what God may be revealing or unveiling for them.' He contrasted this with listening so that *I* can understand what *you* are saying. This was significant because, 'Often, the hardest conversation is the one that you're trying to have with yourself.'

Another idea learnt from Boulding was 'the *two-hundred-year present*'. He explained, 'Reflect on your own family. Which elder held you as a young child when you were born? Then think of yourself as an older person, holding a young child, and the age that child might live to. Suddenly you're easily into two centuries. Now, in this moment, you're living your two-hundred-year present.' It was a beautiful idea, one that connects, I suggested, with breathing deeper, being in less of a rush and getting in touch with something of God's perspective on the present. John Paul agreed, saying, 'That's why, in my work, I seek to avoid being crisis-driven but rather be crisis-responsive. I want to retain a sense of the bigger picture, of where we are headed, and of generational thinking.'

What makes a person an effective peacemaker? 'A key starting place is the saying, "Know thyself." I'd emphasize the capacity for self-reflection, for self-awareness. How you receive the mirror reflections back from the world about who you are and how you're responding, that's core to developing a better capacity to be present with the ambiguities that conflict represents.' What else? 'There are three qualities that I'd point to: humility, patience and vulnerability. These all shape what becomes invitational to others. How you cultivate and teach them – well that's something I've struggled with.' He continued, 'Self-awareness comes from the same root as compassion – with an ability to notice. Noticing is vital. So, when Jesus is walking in a huge crowd, and a woman just touches his clothing, it's his ability to notice that unfolds the story of transformation.' He then concluded, 'I return to saying that it doesn't matter so much what technique you're using or what you say. What really matters is the quality of presence that you bring to a setting.'

Learning from Carolyn Schrock-Shenk

Carolyn Schrock-Shenk was a successor to Lederach as director of Mennonite Conciliation Service. A gifted trainer, she also edited an outstanding collection of resources, prized by others.[2] At the turn of the century, I invited Carolyn to co-lead a week-long mediation and facilitation skills course at the London Mennonite Centre. One incident on the course proved formative for me.

Convinced that power is always a key dimension in understanding any conflict (see Chapter 4), Carolyn had developed a training tool to help course participants reflect on their own power. The facilitator invites people to stand in a line and take a certain number of steps forwards, heel-to-toe, according to the level of personal power they have in various categories. So, for example, if you are male, you are invited to take three steps forward, if female, then one step. Bridge Builders called this 'the power steps exercise'.

Carolyn and I used this exercise early on the second day of our course. By the end of the power steps, the group was dispersed across a typical spread. At the front were two men, and those towards the front were mostly men, with a couple of women. Towards the back were mostly women, although there was one older man there. The penultimate person from the back was the only black person in the group, a younger woman, called Charity.

We next went through a debriefing process, individually and then around tables. After the table conversations, we invited plenary feedback. We began by asking some who ended up at the front to report on their feelings. 'Embarrassed,' said one; 'Awkward and conflicted,' said another. Yet another said, 'If I'm honest, I felt competitive, wondering if I'd end up at the front.' Then we invited expression of feelings from those who ended up towards the back. 'Disheartened,' said one. 'Frustrated,' said another. Then Charity spoke up. 'I felt angry and disturbed,' she said. 'It seemed like all the obstacles I've battled against throughout my life were being thrown back in my face and highlighted before the rest of the group. The exercise compounded my painful experience of racism and gender inequality.' I was unprepared for such a strong reaction; but tried to summarize it. However, I felt uncomfortable and out of my depth in trying to explore the issues being raised. Not so Carolyn, who intervened, piping up, 'Charity, I appreciate your honesty with us. I'd welcome the opportunity to hear more during the next break, if you're willing to share with us.' Charity agreed to do so.

We saw out the rest of the session. At its conclusion, Carolyn made a bee-line for Charity, and I followed in her wake. We found a quiet seat away from the group, in the garden. Carolyn began, 'Please tell us more about how this exercise affected you. I'd appreciate understanding why you reacted so strongly.' We then listened as Charity poured out her concerns and talked about life challenges she had faced. Carolyn kept listening and checking her understanding. I noticed that Carolyn avoided getting defensive; she did not try to justify the exercise, although she did reiterate its intended purpose. It was soon time to begin the next session. But Charity was not finished; so, Carolyn asked me to begin the next session without them. Half-way through the session, the two returned. Charity was noticeably calmer and freer; and able to participate fully in the remainder of the day, and the rest of the course.

I learnt a vital lesson from Carolyn that day: in working with conflict and with strong feelings, we often need to move towards the person articulating the conflict, and to work at listening to them, no matter how uncomfortable it feels. My temptation had been to back off, and to avoid Charity during the break. Carolyn showed me the need to embrace the conflict, to sit in the fire of another's strong feelings, and to keep working at listening to the person's concerns without getting defensive. I saw how important such attentiveness is. It meets a fundamental need we each have to be heard, understood and recognized. I noted that offering this type of deep listening could then help to free up a person to re-engage productively with a larger process, as happened for Charity.

Reflections from Carolyn Schrock-Shenk

When we spoke recently, Carolyn remembered this incident, having stayed in contact with Charity over several years. Reflecting on peacemaking as a skilled craft, Carolyn said, 'I think we're all called to be peacemakers: that's a call to every follower of Jesus. Within that, some are called to an active peacemaking role, and among us are those who are gifted from the outset. However, all of us can grow and improve. Whether it's learning how to connect deeply with people, or listening for the essence of what people need; or whether it's learning how to hold many disparate pieces together all at once, or developing the creativity that's needed – all are aspects of peacemaking you can grow in. And the more you grow, the more you find that you're practising a skilled craft.'

What did she mean by 'listening for the essence'? 'When I teach paraphrasing, I explain that we're listening for the essence of the message that a person is seeking to convey, and then trying to express it in a nutshell. This requires tuning in to the speaker, giving them your full attention. Then you take what you've received and try to name the essence of it. I *love* doing that. When you hear someone respond with "Yes, yes – that's it!" – it can be so powerful, it gives me shivers just describing it.' She added, 'The best gift you can give someone is to help them hear themselves in a different way – in a way that adds more light and understanding to their own reality.' (This resonates with the idea of 'prophetic listening' described by Lederach.)

Carolyn identified Regina Shands Stoltzfus, an African-American Mennonite, as an important influence. 'One gift of the best peacemakers is the capacity to hold together both the pastoral and the prophetic. Not many can. Some are good pastorally, others are good prophetically, but few can hold both together – that's a great gift. Over many years, Regina modelled that for me. I said to myself, "This is the type of peacemaker I want to be." I want to be firmly rooted in justice and right relationships, and in that way be prophetically challenging – but to do so in a way that is deeply respectful and caring of the person. That's a godly combination. That's what I aspire to. But it's hard.'

Conflict engager, or conflict avoider?

Peacemakers with different temperaments can learn much by observing one another. I am a natural 'conflict engager'. Peacemakers of this type are able to face into difficulties. They can 'sit in the fire' and be brave in engaging with painful conflict. Natural conflict engagers often need to learn to pause: to 'put up their sword' and avoid rushing in. Those who are more naturally 'conflict avoiders' can teach them important lessons. Two examples of conflict avoiders come to my mind. One is the mother of an intense young man. When he gets heated, her gentleness and kindness help him to calm down. She is adept at choosing the right moment to explore a thorny issue that needs raising, often initially through a less direct approach. A second example: a work colleague of mine who would set aside his own concerns for the sake of making progress with our work. Without making a fuss, at a later stage he would choose a moment to mention something he had been unhappy about. If not careful, I might miss the importance of attending to him. It always repaid taking the time to listen when he spoke up, offering insight that I would otherwise have missed. Watching such peacemakers can teach those of us who are conflict engagers to hold our tongue, and to wait for the fruitful moment to explore a difficult issue.

Wherever we are on the spectrum between eager conflict engager and dedicated conflict avoider, there will be insights to be learnt from others who are at a different point along the spectrum. (In terms of our natural preferences, there is usually a correlation with the personal styles explored in Chapter 2.) Those who are conflict avoiders will bring gifts of kindness and gentleness, and avoid unnecessary confrontation. For them to grow further, there may be a need to 'polish up their sword', as it were. This means being readier to engage with a conflict and the intensity of others' emotions, journeying with them through the storm. Part of this may be coming to terms with their own difficult feelings, which they may find hard to express or acknowledge.

I asked Carolyn – a natural conflict engager – about this spectrum, and she identified two different types of conflict avoider. 'One kind are those who hate conflict, but then let it fester inside. It makes them resentful, hard to live with – they become bitter complainers. What I've learnt from them is that, if it really bothers you, then you've got to address it.' She continued, 'A different kind are the conflict avoiders who live by grace. They say, "Grace covers it." They don't like something that happened, but they recognize that's how the other person is, and move on. Somehow, they're able to extend grace. From them, I've learnt that not every conflict needs to be challenged and taken on. Sometimes you have to say, "That's just the way it is. I'll let go; and live with that." From them, I'm slowly learning to become more of an extender of grace.'

Sustaining peacemakers

Every experienced peacemaker recognizes that there is a cost to peacemaking. So, I want to say a word on the need for peacemakers to care for themselves. For, as one interviewee put it, 'What you don't pay attention to, will eventually catch up with you.' During my conversation with Joe Campbell, more of which follows, he said the following: 'After a good number of years doing church mediation cases, it was having a negative effect on how I was seeing the Church. Too often I was seeing the dark side of church life; and that became spiritually draining. As mediators, we need to attend to what the work is doing to us. We need to find ways to nurture and encourage our own spirit, as a bulwark against the negativity that can come from the cases that we're handling. Self-care is vital. This matters if we're to be sustained for the long haul.'

John Paul Lederach identified the importance of his family life in providing 'a groundedness in normal life'. Attending a basketball game with one of his children could act as an important counterbalance to the drain of peacebuilding work. Also, spending time in nature and in meditation, walking and reading poetry all help him 'to be the nudge of calm in the midst of the storm'. Carolyn Schrock-Shenk said that knowing her limits, her strengths and when to say 'no' were all important, as well as practising thankfulness: together, these helped to sustain her. If you are involved in active peacemaking work, whether serving within the Church, or as a Christian working in the wider world, you will want to ensure that you have appropriate support in place for yourself, and that you know what sustains and renews you.

John Paul shared this haiku, written while working with a group of mediators in Myanmar: 'Don't ask the mountain to move. Just take a pebble each time you visit.' He commented, 'Being alongside a mountain gives you a great deal of perspective on your place in the world. And when you face a mountain, a monumental, almost impossible task – like peace in Colombia, peace in congregation X, you name it – your perspective can't be, "I've got to go out today and get that mountain to move," your perspective will need to be, "What's my pebble today?"' Then he added, 'And finding a way to stay joyful in the midst of it – there is our challenge.'

A conversation with Joe Campbell

Joe has extensive experience as a mediator and is a former assistant director of Mediation Northern Ireland. He has also worked overseas in Nepal. More recently, he has focused on conflicts in churches and Christian organizations; and he helped to establish the Presbyterian Church of Ireland's Conciliation Service.

How did you come into the field of mediation and into working with conflict in churches?
In one sense it began with burn-out. I ran out of energy and resources after 11 years of frontline youth work in troubled Belfast, starting in the 1970s. So, I had a sabbatical in the USA in 1987–8 at a Mennonite seminary. I took various courses there. I was particularly energized by the opportunity to train and volunteer with a local Victim–Offender Reconciliation Program.

I also attended a week-long mediation skills course. I was excited by what I learnt, because I was still getting over the hurt and anger of past messed-up working relationships. And it was *so* relevant for Northern Ireland, where there was a low-level civil war festering on. Suddenly, it dawned on me that *the Bible had something to say about conflict*: Jesus in his ministry, Paul in his, and the life of the early church – there was so much there about working with conflict. The lights suddenly came on.

When I returned to Northern Ireland, I learnt that three others I knew had also done some mediation training, one a Roman Catholic religious sister. Together, we formed Mediation Network for Northern Ireland. We employed a director and a part-time administrator; and offered training for diverse groups, including a mediation course. Some people turned up on the first night thinking the class was on meditation! The idea of *mediation* hadn't yet sunk into our society.

There were several Presbyterian churches in Ireland facing painful conflicts. Some older ministers were saying, 'It's just the younger ministers coming in and wanting too much change.' Perhaps so, but there were also many other issues. I'd seen Mennonite Conciliation Service's way of working with divided congregations, and we wanted to offer something similar for Presbyterians in Ireland. We recruited about 15 people to train as church mediators. They were lay and clergy, women and men, of various ages, including two retired ministers. We were then invited to mediate church cases. Usually these came to us way too late – some were several years old, festering sores in the lives of those congregations.

We had to reckon with a feeling of *shame* about conflict in the church. People felt that they'd failed God, themselves and their congregation. This meant that mediation was approached with deep reluctance, as a last gasp effort.

Gradually the idea caught on, and cases started to come to us before everything was so entrenched. Overall, we've now handled more than 100. Sometimes it's been what we call 'conflict coun-selling', where one side, such as a minister, elder or deacon, talks through a situation, needing a safe space to process their thinking. Other times, there was a congregational mediation process. Some were focused on in-house church issues: worship styles, property, use of finance or leadership styles. Others concerned a family dispute that had spilled over into the congregation.

Which peacemakers have most influenced you? What have you admired about them?

My grandfather and grandmother impressed me with their courage – the courage to do things differently. When they wed in the early 1900s, they married across the Protestant–Catholic divide. They had 11 children, six girls and five boys. My grandmother, being a Catholic, was required to give an assurance that all the children would be raised Catholic. But my grandparents refused to conform. The boys were brought up Catholic, opposite to the religion of their father. While the girls – my mother included – were brought up Protestant. The sons then married Catholic women, while the daughters married Protestants. Now, over 100 years later, my grandparents' decision has had a profound effect: it's given us a whole raft of both Protestant *and* Catholic cousins, all in one family. So, I'm connected with both communities, and have insights into both. It therefore wasn't chilling for me working with Catholic folk, which it could be for other Protestants, educated in separate schools, living parallel lives.

My mother is another heroine of mine. She had a profound effect on our family. She was the 'go-to' person whenever there were difficulties in a marriage or a dispute of some kind: she was the unofficial family counsellor, because she was such a good listener. She didn't have a job outside the home: her job was being available, which she always was. I admired how she would walk alongside other people.

A key thing I learnt was respect for other people. When working with a dispute, you may know in your core that someone has got it wrong and will have to give ground. But having respect for them is vital. I never heard my mother or grandparents putting others down.

What can help someone grow in the art of peacemaking?
For me, the biblical thread has been important: it continues to inform, excite and lead me. Reconciliation is God's passion: it's not something we need to twist out of the Scriptures, it comes alive on almost every page. I believe it's inherent in who God is.

Reading the Bible the other day, I read a story where Jesus refuses to do a mediation. One brother, in dispute with another, says to Jesus, 'Tell my brother to give me half of the inheritance.' Jesus responds, 'It's not my job to divide that up.' He didn't reject the man; he brought him to a deeper understanding. He was saying, 'It's *your* job to repair your relationship with your brother. Then the money issue will be resolved.' Jesus was pointing to the nub: it isn't about fixing 'the problem', it's about how we address our relationships with one another. Of course, some don't like this challenge: they just want you to sort the problem out. But yet again Jesus says, 'The real issue is how you get along with another brother or sister.' Sometimes that's literally in the same family; just as often it's in the family of God.

I no longer work directly with the Presbyterian Conciliation Service, but I do some mentoring of mediators. Debriefing is so important. As I sit with a pair of mediators who've been involved in a delicate case, a challenging question can sometimes unlock further development – perhaps identifying a mistake made, or an insight gained. I'd go so far as saying, it should be mandatory for mediators to sit with someone to reflect on their practice and go on learning.

What's coming to my mind is a door into a Nepali church. Outside the door are all these pairs of shoes lying around on the ground (because they don't wear shoes into the church building). I sometimes think that being invited into a church's conflict, we almost need to go bare-foot. We need to feel and hear the vibrations and to be respectful of people's situation. I think of God saying to Moses, 'Take off your sandals, the ground you're walking on is holy ground.' Obviously, we need training and we need to gain experience. But that's not all. We also need reliance on the Holy Spirit, who'll be our teacher and guide. Responding to the setting – that's vital.

To me, the sign of a good mediation is where the mediators slip out and the people involved almost believe that they did it all themselves. It's great when that happens. And whenever an agreement is reached in a church that's been in conflict, I find that it's a profound, spiritual experience.

A Theological Reflection:

John 21.15–19 (Jesus restores Peter)

The last encounter in John's Gospel is an exchange between Jesus and Peter revealing something intriguing about Jesus' approach to handling conflict. There is a fraught back story. Peter has made rash promises. Jesus has rebuked him for drawing his sword. Peter has wilted feebly under questioning. Jesus has watched Peter abandoning him to humiliation and horror. Then Jesus has died in agony, and yet has found that death cannot hold him. In anyone's book, that is a lot to go through in a short period: enough, you might think, to blot out what happened on that fateful night in the upper room, garden and courtyard. However, Jesus does not forget Peter's betrayal of him. He also knows that Peter cannot forget his abandonment of Jesus and his failure to stand up and be counted. Where now?

The main events in Jerusalem have passed, some weeks before. Peter and some other disciples have wandered back up north, to Galilee, to somewhere they felt more comfortable – back to their old trade, fishing from small boats. It is early morning. Peter and his friends have been up all night; and caught nothing. A shadowy figure asks what success they have had; then tells them to re-cast their net. Suddenly the fishermen are swamped by an overwhelming catch. This is a déjà-vu moment for Peter (see Luke 5.1–11).

What is Jesus doing there? Only after their breakfast does Peter find out. Jesus invites Peter to walk with him along the shoreline. As Peter discovers, Jesus has come for *that* conversation, the one Peter was hoping to avoid. However, Jesus does not tackle Peter's betrayal directly. He addresses Peter by his birth name and asks a challenging question: 'Simon, son of John, do you love me more than these?' How can Peter answer such a question? How compare his love with that of others? But Peter is also taken back to his own fateful words, 'Even if all abandon you, *I* will never betray you.' There is no hiding. The emptiness of Peter's earlier claim is thrust upon him. He replies feebly, if honestly, 'You know that I care for you.'[3]

However, Jesus isn't done. He asks a second time, 'Do you love me – enough to lay down your life for me?' What can Peter say? He is no longer prepared to overstate matters. 'Lord, you know that I care for you.' But Jesus is not letting Peter off the hook yet. There were three denials. So, there's a third question, 'Do you really care for me?' Peter is cut to the quick, and it hurts. In exasperation he replies, 'Lord, you know everything; you know I care for you.' Peter no longer has any illusions about himself or his love for Jesus. And it is this Peter, shorn of self-delusion, whom Jesus commissions afresh for ministry. Three times Peter hears a call: 'Feed my lambs.' 'Tend my sheep.' 'Feed my sheep.' With the sword of his mouth, combining challenge with caring, Jesus gently but incisively lays bare the limits of Peter's love, and the reality of his failure. With the same sword, he restores Peter to leadership in the community of disciples. And then he twists the sword a final time by revealing that Peter will indeed lay down his life for his Lord (John 21.18).

Like Peter, we are tempted to draw our swords when facing conflict. Like Peter, we can fail Jesus at critical moments. Like Peter, we delude ourselves about the extent of our love for Jesus. But, as with Peter, Jesus can also transfigure our violent tendencies and our failures to love God – sometimes paradoxically, with wounding designed to heal – and can recommission us to work for peace in the service of the Christian community and the wider world. As to Peter, Jesus invites each of us: 'Follow me.'

Notes

1 John Paul Lederach, 2005, *The Moral Imagination: The Art and Soul of Building Peace*, New York, NY: Oxford University Press.

2 Carolyn Schrock-Shenk (ed.), 2004, *Mediation and Facilitation Training Manual: Foundations and Skills for Constructive Conflict Transformation*, Akron, PA: Mennonite Conciliation Service. There were earlier editions, including in 1995 and 1999.

3 I am indebted to Sam Wells for his exposition of the two different kinds of love used in the original Greek: a difference between *philein*, to cherish, and *agapein*, to lay down one's life.

12

Build Bridges to Heaven

This final chapter weaves together a few threads from the conversations with my dialogue partners and interviewees. I have selected some gems that seem significant; and I will offer some consolidating reflections and tell some final stories. Lastly, I will engage in a conversation with Sam Wells, inviting him to cast his response as theological reflection. That is a treat for us to end with.

Unexpected encounter

I begin by wondering about the inter-play between heaven and earth hinted at in an epic biblical story. The story is that of Jacob, Isaac's younger son. It is full of significance as a tale of reconciliation between Jacob and his older brother Esau, and of reconciliation with God.[1] Here, we look at just one unusual incident.

The starting point is grim. Jacob is a thief. He has stolen both the blessing and the birth-right of the firstborn from his older brother. In his fury at being robbed of his inheritance, the older brother exclaims that he will murder Jacob. Jacob panics, and flees from the parental home and country. He is now a refugee on the run. Alone, and out in the wilderness, he is full of fear. He finds himself in the middle of nowhere. Then, exhausted, he lies down to sleep.

Against all his expectations, this proves to be a liminal moment. During the night, when Jacob is no longer in control and his protective shell has slipped, he has a vision of some kind – or is it a dream? He sees a type of pathway connecting earth to heaven. Travelling up and down are message-carriers, bearing missives from God. However, these messengers have nothing for Jacob. Instead, an intimate voice speaks directly to the young renegade. A voice that reveals itself as God's. And God has two messages for Jacob, two words of promise. The first is this: 'I am with you.' The second, which follows close on its tail, is similar: 'I will not leave you' (Gen. 28.15). The next morning, Jacob awakes, his mind blown open. He had thought he was alone. He was worried about whether he would survive in the wilderness, fearful of death. Now, in this empty, nowhere place, he finds that God is present. God is close, and personal. With him. Now. And ahead. Jacob expresses his mind-expanding discovery this way: 'Heaven's doors are open.'

When we are in the midst of a painful human conflict, we can find that Jacob's story is our story. We may find ourselves deeply confused, feeling lost and isolated. We may be regretting things we have said or done. Or, we may be bemoaning how others have treated us. It can feel like a wilderness. We may even wonder whether life is worth living. And then, when least expected, we find that God is close. Gently whispering to us, 'I am with you.' God knows that, at a deep level, we fear abandonment; knows that we are unsure who our friends are. And the voice comes again: 'I will not leave you.'

Times of conflict can bring such moments of revelation. We discover that God – the God of Jacob – is with us; and will never abandon us. Despite what appears to be contradictory evidence, we find that there is a place of welcome for us with God. Heaven's doors are open – open for us. And what is more, we learn that there is a community of fellow strugglers for us to belong to, waiting for us to join them. Such discoveries are the witness of those who have journeyed into and through human conflicts. And peacemakers who walk alongside such strugglers find that they share in the discovery. This can be, as Sandra Cobbin said, the 'nugget of gold' amidst conflict.

Holy ground

It should not be surprising, therefore, that working with people embroiled in a painful conflict requires us to recognize 'holy ground', as Joe Campbell described it. Hence, we need to walk 'bare-foot', with great sensitivity, and with courage. I think of one priest who came to see me over the course of many months while facing protracted conflict within his church. The situation took such a toll that he set himself a date by which he would resign his position: he thought he could keep going in the short term, if he could envisage an end. He was often in tears during his consultation sessions. Tears of pain, frustration and helplessness. Tears of despair at the lack of love he experienced, and his own lack of love for those he was shepherding. As we teased out the tangled mess that he sought to unravel during our conversations, I found myself metaphorically holding my breath, walking the fine line between being supportive and appropriately challenging. I sensed his own fragility and that of his community. We were indeed treading holy ground. For he was seeking to discern whether they really were all held in God's loving hands, amidst their intense frictions and anxieties; and, if so, how he could move forward with his flock, as their pastor. He needed a bridge to heaven.

All I could offer this priest was accompaniment along the journey, and a space to be heard and metaphorically held. That meant being comfortable with *silence*, and with not having the answers for him. This is important for the work of peacemaking. There is no substitute to enjoying 'the gift of silence', as Frank White called it, where we are simply present and attentive to God. This involves becoming people for whom 'silence is a trusted friend'; and who, even when we are with others, can enjoy 'companionable silence' with them. The contemplative traditions have much to teach us here, among them the monastic communities, the Quakers, and the newer monastics, such as the Taizé community. They are communities where we can encounter God in the midst of collective silence; and, from this, grow into a calmer presence with others.

Hope-bringers

For those called to walk alongside others in their conflicts, a recurring theme in my interviews was the need for *hope*. Carolyn Schrock-Shenk said she saw herself as 'a hope-bringer' for people mired in a conflict; another interviewee spoke of being 'a hope-bearer' for conflicted churches. John Paul Lederach saw his international peacebuilding work bringing 'a sense of hope' that repeated destructive patterns might be broken, and a new way found for people to live together. Such work calls for imagination and creativity. It also requires being grounded in a story that can act as an 'anchor of the soul' (Heb. 6.19). Without such anchorage, peacemakers will find it hard to sustain their ministry to others who have lost hope – if only for a season – especially if those people are fellow believers feeling guilty about being in despair.

I recall a Christian congregation that I once worked with. I can still see the pained faces of the lay leaders at the outset: they had lost hope for their church and its future. They were struggling to imagine a way through their entanglements after the departure of a long-standing minister, and the sudden appearance of a major cleft within the group. They felt as if their church was adrift on a stormy sea, having lost its anchor, with the waves breaking over their little boat. And their basic message to us mediators was, 'Save us, we're sinking.' However, we had no lifeboats and certainly no magic wands. And, unlike Jesus, we had no power to rebuke the wind and still the waves (Matt. 8.26). What we did have was the confidence that, working together, we could find a way to bring clarity to the issues they faced. And we believed it was possible to restore more open, honest relationships. These would need to be grounded in critical self-reflection, and a move away from finger-pointing. Just as importantly, we had a conviction, based on our trust in God and our reflection on God's story, that the Holy Spirit could restore their hope over the course of a journey with us. That confidence gave them a glimmer of light.

It soon became clear that this church community was close to splitting apart. As we worked together, we helped to build a more complex picture of what had led up to the current spike of tensions, and to expose the deeper roots. These lay in a range of historic hurts, going back several decades, hurts that could only be shared in a safe space. We hosted small groups where every participant had some uninterrupted time to share their perspective, and to unburden their concerns. Later, the mediators presented an interim report painting a wide canvas, and one could sense the anxiety in the group dropping. They were, in Sarah Hills' words, finding calmer places of greener pasture and stiller water. Over several months, the mediators noticed hope gradually beginning to return. This was reflected in a 'metaphors exercise' late in the mediation process.

We identified some images that resonated widely within the group. One was a crumbling fortress with the drawbridge raised up: it was a metaphor of their church as a closed community caught up with internal feuding, which new and marginal people found it difficult to feel part of. It was a searingly honest image, giving food for thought. At a subsequent session, we looked at how participants could envision the earlier images being transformed. One person drew a picture of a shining temple with feasting tables on the streets outside: a metaphor of their church as a place of unexpected welcome, attracting a huge diversity of people. Unconsciously – but perhaps unsurprisingly – it was an image of heaven. And together we explored how this vision of their church could become a reality.

One reason this church had decided to employ mediators was that they wanted to be more attractive to any potential new minister. Word had got out about their conflicts! So, they wanted news to spread that they had worked at reconciliation together. It did seem likely that this would appeal to prospective ministerial candidates. So, it was a surprise to receive an invitation to the appointment of their next minister – a full seven years later. At the reception after the institution service, I asked the lay leaders why it had taken so long to find a new minister. There were various reasons. But one thing was both striking and heartening: 'We wouldn't have made it through these last seven years, united as a body, if we hadn't undertaken that bridge-building journey.' They continued, 'It gave us the hope and confidence to keep travelling together.' I was encouraged that Bridge Builders had helped to create a place of 'safe human encounter amidst differences' – Rachel Treweek's words – which placed 'a high value on relationship even in a place of vehement disagreement'. Their work of bridge-building sustained them for the unforeseen seven long years of waiting.

Work in progress

I wonder what has struck you as you have read this book. I hope you are embracing the call to travel on a journey of growth into greater maturity. As Liz Holdsworth put it, this is about finding a place where we are 'both individually distinct from, as well as emotionally connected with others – a balanced place between the competing forces of togetherness and separateness'. And there is a paradox here: focusing on oneself in this way 'turns out to be an unselfish act'. Time and again, interviewees remarked that peacemakers need to grow in self-awareness and self-understanding if they are to be effective in serving others. John Paul Lederach went even further: 'To be a peacemaker, a key is your ability to fully live into the things that you're inviting others to do.' Or, as the Quakers put it: 'Let your life speak.'

I also wonder what you see as 'work in progress' for you and your church community, in relating to one another. We have looked at some challenging questions. How do we understand and appreciate those different from us? When tensions arise between us, how do we find a way to address them? When hurt by someone else, how do we overcome that hurt, and move beyond seeing another person as our 'enemy'? Are there limits to the hurt that can be overcome? At root, these are all about: our relationships and their complexities in the light of our past experience of hurt and managing anxiety; how we understand ourselves in relation to God; and the type of relationships that God invites us into. There is no pretence that this is easy. For, as Justin Welby, the current Archbishop of Canterbury, has said, 'How we live with our deepest differences is probably the fundamental challenge of our time – for the world as well as the Church.'[2]

Glimpsing heaven on earth

If we are to be part of God's people, then we are called to find ways to build bridges with one another, bridges that straddle our anxiety and cross over our differences, bridges that move us beyond our hurts. Doing so requires us to face and understand ourselves anew, stripped of the illusions that we each carry about ourselves.[3] It demands that we look afresh at those who make us uncomfortable – or who have unjustly injured us. And it will cause us to reconsider the scope of God's love, and what it means to truly follow Jesus' example.

Why might we want to work at all this in a special way within the Christian community, within the Church? One who devoted his life to working for reconciliation among Christians of different traditions was Roger Schütz, better known as Brother Roger of Taizé. For Brother Roger, 'It was the vision of the reconciliation of the whole of humanity which made the effort of striving for reconciliation between Christians worthwhile.'[4] I am with Brother Roger. The work of bridge-building within the Church is worth investing in. It is even worth devoting one's life to. Because it is about seeking to win a glimpse of heaven on earth, for the sake of humankind.

We cannot pretend that there are not forces ranged against us, 'the cosmic powers of this present darkness' (Eph. 6.12). Those are evident in the systemic struggles that we face. Ultimately, however, thanks to God's good grace in Jesus, while our efforts at bridge-building may sometimes fail, they will never be in vain. For we are destined for a peace-filled, conflict-transfigured heavenly community, where we will bring all our gifts and creativity to addressing all our diversity and differences. We are destined for a place where we will make peace with the conflict within ourselves and in our relationships with others. A place where we are gently held in the love of God, gathered around Jesus Christ in worship, inspired by the Holy Spirit, and finally reconciled to our trinitarian God. A place called heaven. I hope that you will join me and my fellow bridge-builders, as we seek to bring a taste of that heaven here on earth – in the Church, and beyond.

A conversation with and theological reflection by Sam Wells

Sam is a preacher, pastor, writer, broadcaster and theologian. He has served as a Church of England parish priest for over 20 years and has been the Vicar of St Martin-in-the-Fields since 2012. He has published extensively and is a visiting professor of Christian ethics at King's College, London.

In what ways do you see yourself having been involved in 'bridge-building' as a pastor and parish priest?
I see the Christian life as being with God, oneself, one another, and the creation. Waking up and coming to one's senses, as the prodigal son did in the pigsty, means recognizing the extent to which one is alienated, and in greater or lesser degree antagonized, from each of those four. Thus salvation, mission, reconciliation, healing and peace are all ultimately the same thing.

The work of being able to be with God is possible because God in Christ has overcome all that stands between us. Becoming a Christian is thus accepting the fact that God has done this and letting the Holy Spirit shape one's life in accordance with the way God does this. This is what is usually called salvation, although the way I've described it makes clear that salvation is a process of reconciliation.

Mission is seeking to extend that reconciliation with God, to other people and to the creation. Like salvation, it begins with recognizing a condition of alienation and sometimes enmity. Reconciliation isn't a possession that 'I' have and 'you' lack. Sharing faith therefore isn't about transferring a body of information from me to you, it's about inviting you on a path of reconciliation.

As a pastor and parish priest I'm trying to forge a community of hope that lives in the freedom from fear offered by the promise of resurrection and the relief from regret bestowed by the forgiveness of sins. Almost every human interaction requires some degree of reconciliation, because it usually starts from a position of some degree of alienation or antagonism. And that alienation or antagonism invariably lies in some form of hiatus in relation to oneself, to God, or to the creation. If we regard bridge-building as a metaphor for reconciliation, then it characterizes almost all of my work as a parish priest – whether in pastoral care, worship, preaching, Christian formation, community engagement, leadership, evangelism, or fellowship.

Why do you think people struggle so much with building bridges with one another, across their differences and divisions? Why is it so hard?

In 1915 the American physiologist Walter Bradford Cannon coined the term 'fight or flight' to describe how the nervous system of an animal's body responds to threats. More recently, physiologists talk of a third instinctive response, known as 'freeze'. These three terms readily apply to the experience of parish life. Very often people see a local church as a place in and community through which to discharge frustrations accumulated elsewhere. If they feel they can win, they fight; if they doubt they can win, they flee; and if they've been living with the issues a long time, they may be inclined to freeze. The gospel invites us to take a different path in the face of discord: what Ephesians 6 calls 'standing firm'. Standing firm means recognizing our differences from one another, but trying to avoid those differences evoking tension, never mistaking tension for conflict, and refusing to let conflict turn into violence or war.

The simplest, but most deeply flawed, response to the tension that can arise from difference is to try to surround oneself with sameness – as if the problem were difference, and by eradicating difference one eradicated tension. This is many kinds of wrong. It's wrong because one will invariably begin to find differences with even the most similar people if they're the only ones left with whom to disagree. It's wrong because difference is a created good – God made us and intended us to be different from one another, and the secret is not to abolish difference, but to use all the diverse gifts of God's creation to the full; and if we fail to do so and experience our lives as scarcity then we have only ourselves to blame. Most of all it's wrong because the Holy Trinity is itself diverse: the community of Father, Son and Holy Spirit, three in one and one in three, shows that even in the heart of God there is difference, and that difference is an expression of perfection, not of deficit.

The irony is that many people's notion of peace is of an existence without difference and tension. But such an expectation is fertile ground for the emergence of conflict, violence, and war.

What do you see as the relationship between the work of transforming conflict, the craft of making peace and the good news about Jesus Christ?

They're all more or less the same. It's common to see the work of a priest as the highest calling; but, for me, the work of a conciliator in peace talks, of a marriage guidance counsellor, or a restorative justice facilitator is about the closest we get to the work of Christ. I've been influenced by the work of Ched Myers and Elaine Enns in distinguishing between peacebuilding, peacemaking, peacekeeping and peacewaging – particularly the way they highlight how the appropriate approach differs depending on the power balance in play.[5] But more broadly, I understand peace not as a state to be attained but as a process to be entered into. All of us are addicted to the fight–flight–freeze responses, so all of us are in 'recovery' and thus at some stage or other along a 12-step path. I name the 12 steps as follows:

1. *Resolve* – where you recognize that you're better than the person you've become, mired in conflict.

2. *Ceasefire* – not the end of hatred, but the conclusion of acts of war.

3. *Account* – the telling of a truthful story of how you got to this place.

4. *Apology* – acknowledgement of responsibility and genuine sorrow for the significant hurt, irreplaceable damage and wrong intention.

5. *Penance* – tangible recompense and active quest to understand one's wrong actions.

6. *Agreement* – an understanding about how things will be from now on, averting the circumstances and discouraging the behaviours that gave rise to the conflict.

7. *Repentance* – recognition of the depth of the problem and commitment never to let such circumstances arise again.

8. *Confession* – full, final, and exhaustive articulation of specific acts of wrongdoing.

9. *Forgiveness* – a decision not to be defined by resentment or antagonism, to seek a bigger life than one constantly overshadowed by this painful story, and to allow one's perception of the harm received no longer to stand in highlighted isolation but to blend slowly into the myriad of wrongs and griefs to which the world has been subject across time.

10. *Reconciliation* – discovering that the former enemy has part of the key to one's own flourishing without which one will remain in some sense still in the prison of hatred.

11. *Healing* – realizing one's life is no longer dominated by enmity, discovering wisdom and relationship that would not otherwise have been so, and perceiving in this benighted period a source of compassion, dignity and hope.

12. *Resurrection* – the resurrection of Jesus – the body raised, and the forgiveness, resurrection and healing entailed – is precisely an account of what peace entails.

Note that the first six are broadly secular, the last six evidently Christian, and in particular the last two are explicitly acts of the Holy Spirit and not ourselves.

What might an understanding of God as bridge-builder mean for us in being faithful Christian disciples and sharers of the gospel in our world?

The tendency is to see reconciliation either as exasperating, because if Christ has come all argument should have ceased, or as wasteful, because it uses up precious time that could be better spent evangelizing or bringing salvation in some other way. The revolution comes in seeing that God's whole life is shaped towards reconciling: every action of God is in restoring the world to full communion – so we may be with God, ourselves, one another and the creation, on earth as in heaven. Only at this point does one realize that reconciliation is the gospel – not a preparation for it or a distraction from it but the very gospel itself. All the other things we might want to do instead of reconciliation are in reality just more amenable forms of reconciliation, attractive because we perceive our chances of success are better than in the intractable case we desire to be diverted from.

Once we appreciate this not only do our humble efforts in mission and ministry become part of the glory of the communion of saints; we realize they are none other than the very work of the Holy Spirit.

Notes

1 For one outstanding reflection, see: John Paul Lederach, 2014, *Reconcile: Conflict Transformation for Ordinary Christians*, Harrisonburg, VA: Herald Press, pp. 29–43.

2 In the foreword to: Phil Groves and Angharad Parry Jones, 2014, *Living Reconciliation*, London: SPCK, p. xii.

3 For more on this, see: Dietrich Bonhoeffer, 2015 (1939), *Life Together*, London: SCM Press.

4 Kathryn Spink, 2015, *A Universal Heart: The Life and Vision of Brother Roger of Taizé*, London: SPCK, p. 134.

5 Elaine Enns and Ched Myers, 2009, *Ambassadors of Reconciliation – Volume Two: Diverse Practices of Restorative Justice and Peacemaking*, Maryknoll, NY: Orbis.

Further Resources

This book is best read in conversation with others. Questions for reflection and small group discussion are therefore available on my website at www.alastairmckay.com/writing.

For those interested in practical training to enhance learning from this book, I recommend Bridge Builders' courses. See: www.bbministries.org.uk. A consortium of UK organizations offering related training are currently collaborating on the 'Reconcilers Together' project. This includes five physical centres and three different services, of which Bridge Builders is one. See: www.reconcilerstogether.co.uk.

A published training resource provides all the materials for leading a nine-session course in your own context. This is aimed at those who have completed foundational training with Bridge Builders. See Alastair McKay, 2015, *Growing Bridgebuilders: Changing How We Handle Conflict*, Coventry: CPAS and Bridge Builders Ministries. Available for purchase from: www.cpas.org.uk/church-resources/growing-bridgebuilders/.

Those interested in an academic presentation of related material might appreciate my doctoral dissertation, 'Practising Oversight, Friendship and Reconciliation in Church Staff Teams: A Case Study of How the Staff Teams of Two Large Anglican Churches Dealt with Disagreement in Team Meetings'. This includes an extensive bibliography and, in Appendix 1, a wide survey of literature relating to church conflict. Free to download at: http://www.alastairmckay.com/writing. The notes at the end of each chapter of this book provide some pointers.